An Introduction to Nursing Informatics

Informatics

Evolution & Innovation

Edited by

Susan M. Houston, MBA, RN-BC, PMP,
CPHIMS, FHIMSS

Tina Dieckhaus, MSN, RN-BC, NE-BC,
CPHIMS, FHIMSS

Bob Kirchner, MSN, MBA/HCM, RN

Renee Rookwood, MS, RN

HIMSS Mission

Globally, lead endeavors optimizing health engagements and care outcomes through information technology.

Printed in the U.S.A. 5 4 3 2 1

Requests for permission to make copies of any part of this work should be sent to:

Permissions Editor
HIMSS
33 W. Monroe St., #1700
Chicago, IL 60603-5616
matthew.schlossberg@himssmedia.com

ISBN: 978-1-938904-82-0

The inclusion of an organization name, product or service in this publication should not be considered as an endorsement of such organization, product or service, nor is the failure to include an organization name, product or service to be construed as disapproval.

For more information about HIMSS, please visit www.himss.org.

About the Editors

Susan M. Houston, MBA, RN-BC, PMP, CPHIMS, FHIMSS, is Chief, Portfolio Office within the Department of Clinical Research Informatics at the National Institutes of Health Clinical Center. Her background includes clinical nursing, informatics, and project and portfolio management. Ms. Houston has presented at the local, regional and national levels. She has authored a variety of articles and books on project management and informatics. She is a member of Project Management Institute (PMI), American Nursing Informatics Association (ANIA), and the Healthcare Information and Management Systems Society (HIMSS), while serving on various committees.

Tina Dieckhaus, MSN, RN-BC, NE-BC, CPHIMS, FHIMSS, is currently the Director for Patient Care Services Informatics at St. Jude Children's Research Hospital. She has 14 years of clinical nursing experience and has been practicing informatics nursing since 1997. Ms. Dieckhaus received her Bachelor's Degree in Nursing from Mississippi University for Women and her Master's Degree in Nursing Informatics from Tennessee State University. She is certified by the ANA as both an Informatics Nurse Specialist and a Nurse Executive. Ms. Dieckhaus is certified as a Certified Professional in Health Information Management Systems and a Fellow of HIMSS.

Bob Kirchner, MSN, MBA/HCM, RN, has been an Informatics Nurse Specialist at Mayo Clinic since 2007. He obtained his BSN from San Jose State University and his MSN and MBA from University of Phoenix. He has 30 years of experience in general care and ICU nursing. Mr. Kirchner was the Nursing Informatics Lead working on the Barcode

Medication Administration project at Mayo Clinic and other point of care documentation projects. He has also served on the HIMSS Nursing Informatics Committee and was the Chairperson for the Nursing Informatics Awareness Workgroup.

Renee Rookwood, MS, RN, as a healthcare advisor, had a passion for informatics that led her to develop a special interest in automating clinical quality measures as well as data analytics in support of hidden, actionable patient safety insights. She holds a Bachelor's of Science in Nursing from James Madison University and a Master's of Science in Health Informatics from George Mason University. Since July 2013, Ms. Rookwood has been the Chair of the HIMSS Nursing Informatics Committee Task Force.

About the Contributors

Lou Barr, MSN/MHA, RN, has been in the medical field for 14 years. He started as a secretary in the emergency department. He graduated from nursing school in 2004 and became an emergency department nurse. Currently, Mr. Barr trains multidisciplinary medical professionals how to navigate and document in St. Jude's electronic medical record.

Charles M. Boicey, MS, RN-BC, PMP, CLNC, CPHIMS, is the Enterprise Analytics Architect for Stony Brook Medicine. He is responsible for the development of enterprise analytics solutions. He is certified in Nursing Informatics, PMP and CPHIMS. Mr. Boicey is the Vice President of the American Nursing Informatics Association and a member of the HIMSS Innovation Committee.

Lisa Anne Bove, DNP, RN-BC, is a Nursing Informatics Specialist focused on improving health through the use of electronic information. She is an active member of HIMSS, the American Nursing Informatics Association and local informatics nursing groups. Dr. Bove has taught informatics at the University of Maryland and has published and spoken on numerous topics, including informatics and project management.

Susan Brown, MSN, FNP-BC, CPHIMS, has been a Family Nurse Practitioner for 20 years. In addition to her certification as an FNP, Ms. Brown is also certified in Nursing Professional Development, and is a Certified Professional in Healthcare Information and Management Systems. Her professional practice experience includes academic faculty, rural primary care, student health, urgent care, nursing professional development, and for the past 10 years, retail health. Currently, Ms. Brown is the Director of Clinical Informatics for CVS/MinuteClinic.

Patricia Foley Daly, DNP, RN-BC, is a Senior Director at Cerner Corp. in Kansas City, MO. Ms. Daly joined Cerner in May 1989. She has served in many nursing roles throughout the organization. She has presented various topics on nursing informatics in academic, national and international settings. Ms. Daly received her BSN degree in nursing in 1978 from the University of San Francisco; her MN from the University of Kansas in 1984; her post Masters Certificate Program in Heath Care Informatics at the University of Kansas in 2011; and her DNP at the University of Kansas in 2014. She is accredited in Nursing Informatics by the ANA. Ms. Daly is a member of HIMSS, ANA, AMIA, Sigma Theta Tau and Phi Kappa Phi. She is currently a member of the HIMSS Nursing Informatics Committee.

Beth L. Elias, PhD, MS, is Adjunct Associate Professor at the Virginia Commonwealth University School of Nursing in Richmond. A previous senior computer systems engineer with experience in health IT, Dr. Elias has been involved in efforts to integrate radiologic imaging services and IT, manage clinical trials patient data, and evaluate next-generation point-of-care testing devices. Dr. Elias has focused on supporting the use of health IT as part of nursing practice. With nurses making up the largest group of health IT users, Dr. Elias feels that these tools should be more effectively integrated into nursing workflow.

Willa Fields, RN, DNSc, FHIMSS, is a Professor in the School of Nursing at San Diego State University. Dr. Fields teaches courses in informatics, performance improvement and healthcare policy. She also consults at Sharp Grossmont Hospital in San Diego County where she helps nursing staff with their projects and publications. Prior to her faculty position, Dr. Fields was the Vice President of Patient Care Systems in the Information Systems Department at Sharp HealthCare, an integrated delivery system in San Diego. Dr. Fields has a diverse background in clinical nursing, education, research, performance improvement, management, and information systems. Her research area of interest is exploration of practices and tools that improve patient safety and the provision of patient care. Dr. Fields is a past Chairwoman of the HIMSS Board of Directors, and was awarded the HIMSS 2013 Nursing Informatics Leadership Award.

Linda Fischetti, MS, RN, is a Department Head for Health Policy, Informatics, Health Information Technology, Economics and Quality at MITRE Corporation. Prior to joining MITRE, she focused on healthcare payment reform and health informatics.

Sarah Knapfel, BSN, RN, CCRN, MSN, is currently the project coordinator for the i-TEAM Grant Program in the College of Nursing at the University of Colorado, Denver. She has several years of clinical intensive care experience, most specifically in the neurosurgical setting. Ms. Knapfel recently completed a Master of Science in Nursing degree with a Healthcare Informatics focus at the University of Colorado.

Kimberly Ellis Krakowski, MSN, RN, CAHIMS, is the Director of Informatics and Innovation for Inova Health System. An expert in performance improvement, Ms. Krakowski is responsible for the ongoing evaluation of enterprise solutions to improve workflow, affordability, quality, and safety. She is a member of the CMS/ONC 2014 Kaizen: Annual Measure Update Workgroup, HIMSS and AONE.

Kathy Lesh, PhD, EdM, MS, RN-BC, a healthcare consultant with MITRE, has more than 30 years of healthcare experience in a variety of positions and settings. Dr. Lesh is certified in Nursing Informatics, has an MS in Nursing from the University of Illinois at Chicago, and a PhD in Human Services from Capella University.

Susan McBride, PhD, RN-BC, CPHIMS, is Professor within the Texas Tech University Health Sciences Center with a research focus on methods development for implementing, evaluating and utilizing EHRs and large healthcare datasets. Teaching responsibilities include graduate courses in statistics, informatics and epidemiology.

Rhelinda McFadden, RN, CPHIT, CPEHR, is a quality specialist nurse and Patient-Centered Medical Home (PCMH) clinical lead for the Arkansas Foundation for Medical Care. She has more than 20 years of healthcare experience, with 10 years in healthcare quality improvement focused specifically on EHR functionality and improving outcomes in primary care physician practices.

Grischa Metlay, PhD, is a Senior Health Policy Analyst at MITRE Corporation, where he works on projects related to Medicare's Value-Based Purchasing programs. Before coming to MITRE, Dr. Metlay received his doctorate from Harvard's History of Science department, with an emphasis on the history of 20th century American health policy.

Patricia Mook, MSN, RN, NEA-BC, is the CNIO for Inova Health System. She is a seasoned executive, working with the CMIO/CIO/CNO, assisting in planning/execution of clinical IT strategies. Ms. Mook provides clinical IT leadership to the operations and IT teams, assisting clinicians in the delivery of efficient and effective patient care leveraging health information technology.

Judy Murphy, RN, FACMI, FHIMSS, FAAN, is CNO and Director, Global Business Services at IBM Healthcare. Prior to this she was CNO and Director-Clinical Quality and Safety, and Deputy National Coordinator for Programs and Policy at the Office of the National Coordinator in Washington, DC. Ms. Murphy's previous 25 years of health informatics experience were at Aurora Health Care in Wisconsin, including the last 10 years as VP-EHR Applications in IT.

Susan K. Newbold, PhD, RN-BC, FAAN, FHIMSS, CHTS-CP, is an educator and consultant in healthcare informatics. Identified as a pioneer in nursing informatics, Dr. Newbold co-edited five books and has written numerous articles on informatics. She has consulted in informatics in the United States, Australia, Canada, New Zealand, Qatar, Singapore, Slovenia and Taiwan. Dr. Newbold presents on many topics related to the use of technology in healthcare and founded a nursing informatics group in 1982.

Sejal Patel, PhD, is a Senior Health Policy Analyst at MITRE Corporation, where she supports the Centers for Medicare & Medicaid Services' strategic planning in healthcare and health IT. Prior to MITRE, she served as senior research historian at the National Institutes of Health. Dr. Patel received her PhD from the University of Pennsylvania in the History and Sociology of Science.

Minnie Raju, MS, RN, is a Clinical Nurse Informaticist with the Department of Clinical Research Informatics at the National Institutes of Health Clinical Center. She holds a Master's Degree in Nursing Informatics from the University of Maryland Baltimore School of Nursing. Ms. Raju's experience includes 17 years in nursing as a Registered Nurse in critical care, management and education. As an informaticist she leads a team that develops and implements numerous electronic documents for the EHR system, improving interdisciplinary clinical workflow supporting clinical care and research.

Darryl W. Roberts, PhD, MS, RN, is a healthcare leader and collaborator in an array of individual and ecological research and evaluation topics, including health IT/informatics; quality improvement, measurement, and management; value-based purchasing; clinical effectiveness; pharmacoeconomics; social policy; and social media influence. Dr. Roberts is a Registered Nurse with 25 years of clinical, informatics, research, management and education experience. He also is an interdisciplinary evaluation scientist focusing on public policy in informatics, quality and clinical arenas. Dr. Roberts is currently a Senior Social Scientist with Econometrica Inc., in Bethesda, MD, and a Principal Consultant at DWResearch & Education Consulting in Washington, DC.

Sylvia Rowe, MSN, RN-BC, LNHA, is Vice President of Clinical Informatics, Ethica Health and Retirement Communities. She obtained her BSN from Georgia College and State University, and her MSN in Informatics from Walden University. She has more than 20 years of experience in long-term care.

Joyce Sensmeier, MS, RN-BC, CPHIMS, FHIMSS, FAAN, is Vice President of Informatics at HIMSS, where she is responsible for clinical informatics, standards and interoperability programs and initiatives.

An internationally recognized speaker and author, Ms. Sensmeier was inducted in 2010 as a Fellow in the American Academy of Nursing.

Mark D. Sugrue, RN-BC, FHIMSS, CPHIMS, is the Chief Nursing Informatics Officer at Lahey Hospital and Medical Center in Burlington, MA, where he is responsible for all current and future state technology to support the delivery of exceptional nursing care. He is recognized nationally for his expertise in patient safety, clinical systems, HIPAA, ARRA/HITECH and the revenue cycle. Mr. Sugrue is an author and a frequent speaker at trade shows and professional conventions.

Acknowledgments

This book is for all the nurses whose focus is on the health of patients and comfort of families, either directly or indirectly. Your title or role is irrelevant, as the profession as a whole is here to improve health and provide comfort. This is a noble and heroic profession. Thank you to those who came before me and those who will follow.
—*Susan M. Houston, MBA, RN-BC, PMP, CPHIMS, FHIMSS*

I want to specifically thank all of the individuals who drew on their personal experiences to make this book a rich picture of the scope and breadth of nursing informatics. Without your history and experiences, future nursing informatics specialists would have nothing to build upon. Thanks for all you have done and will do to make our specialty great.
—*Tina Dieckhaus, MSN, RN-BC, NE-BC, CPHIMS, FHIMSS*

I would like to thank all of the informatics nurses that blazed the path in creating this nursing discipline. Without all of their hard work and dedication nursing informatics would not be where it is today.
—*Bob Kirchner, MSN, MBA/HCM, RN*

As a new editor, one of the most remarkable observations I have made through this process is the comradery nurses bring to any table, including the book authoring forum. An idea is voiced and you have nurses willing to step in and help—whether it is authoring a chapter, seeking out additional contributors, being subject matter experts, or cheerleading us to the finish line—nurses exude teamwork. And so it is poignant to be acknowledging teamwork as the nursing informati-

Table of Contents

Lisa Anne Bove, DNP, RN-BC

Policy Analyst
Darryl W. Roberts, PhD, MS, RN

Former Deputy National Coordinator, Office of the
National Coordinator for Health IT
Judy Murphy, RN, FACMI, FHIMSS, FAAN

Willa Fields, RN, DNSc, FHIMSS

Foreword

Joyce Sensmeier, MS, RN-BC, CPHIMS, FHIMSS, FAAN

As I reviewed this book, I could easily envision the decades of my career passing by. Moving from novice to expert as part of an ever-evolving specialty has certainly had its challenges. But establishing a new specialty in nursing was also an interesting and rewarding process. It is hard to imagine today how we could possibly realize the promise of health IT without informatics nurses at the core of these advancements. And now we are at the cusp of transforming health and healthcare through the many contributions of nursing informatics (NI). As you will discover in this book, informatics nurses are doing exciting and innovative work such as optimizing systems, designing wearable devices, analyzing data to improve health outcomes, and influencing policy.

The authors of this book have clearly described the evolution of NI from our first attempts to define what it was, to our current practice in today's complex, diverse healthcare environment. Many of us began working in informatics roles before we even knew what to name our job titles. And according to the book's first chapter, it appears that some are still struggling with that challenge today. But experiencing 'a day in the life' through the eyes of a variety of informatics nurses as described in the book's last chapter should help the next generation gain a better understanding of what informatics is, and envision the exciting opportunities that lie ahead.

Taking the time to look back over the decades while reviewing the second chapter of this book has helped me to more clearly appreciate the contributions of the NI pioneers, and the communities and resources we have built along the way. Since its inception in the year 2000, the HIMSS Nursing Informatics Community has been thriving, currently representing more than 6,000 informatics nurses. Building on the foundation laid by the Midwest Alliance for Nursing Informatics, which was my very first NI community, HIMSS has advanced NI practice, education and practical research by realizing a cohesive voice for the NI Community and providing strategic guidance and tactical support for its programs and activities.

To add a bit more detail, the HIMSS NI Community focuses on the following objectives:

- Provide domain expertise, leadership and guidance to HIMSS activities, initiatives and collaborations within the specialty of nursing informatics.
- Participate in the Alliance for Nursing Informatics (ANI) to build and sustain a unified voice and to advocate for and achieve the goals of the NI Community.
- Create opportunities to collaborate and partner with other nursing groups to evolve and build a nursing informatics knowledge repository.
- Provide strategic guidance for the programs and activities of the NI Community.
- Serve as a trusted source for NI knowledge, leadership and education and broaden recognition of the key role that informatics nurses play in successful system selection, development, implementation, evaluation and optimization.
- Advise HIMSS Board of Directors on initiatives within the scope of NI practice such as consumer engagement, interprofessional collaboration, and public policy.

Advancing the HIMSS NI Community's vision, scope, and impact represents the most satisfying accomplishment of my career. Being able to partner with other informatics leaders to launch ANI, establish and evolve the TIGER (Technology Informatics Guiding Education Reform) Initiative, contribute to our body of research through the tri-annual HIMSS Nursing Informatics Workforce Survey, implement the CPHIMS certification program, form new collaborations, and develop tools, resources and education for informatics nurses at all phases of their career has offered me an amazing network of colleagues around the globe.

For those of you who may be embarking on a new career in nursing informatics, or if you are beginning to explore this career path, I hope this book will encourage you to take the leap. If you do, what you will discover is the most welcoming group of individuals who are willing and able to mentor you; individuals who will invite you to work alongside them to make a difference in healthcare. Some of these forward-thinking individuals have progressed in their informatics roles through on-the-job training and grassroots experience. Others have taken advantage of some of the formal informatics educational programs available today. But each has demonstrated their leadership qualities by willingly sharing their vision, passion, and commitment to improving health and healthcare.

As we have learned from the Institute of Medicine's (IOM) *Future of Nursing: Leading Change, Advancing Health* report, strong nursing leadership is required to realize the vision of a transformed healthcare system. Although not every nurse begins his or her career with thoughts of becoming a leader, all nurses must be leaders in the design, implementation, and evaluation of the ongoing reforms to the health system. Nurses must understand that their leadership is as important to providing quality care as is their technical ability to deliver care in a safe and effective manner.

Increasingly, informatics nurses are serving in leadership roles in a variety of settings including executive roles in healthcare provider organizations, not-for-profit associations, government agencies, and health IT supplier organizations. Simply put, informatics nurses are leaders, and many are being recognized as Fellows in the American Academy of Nursing, the highest honor in the nursing profession.

The scope of NI is ever-evolving. The American Nurses Association's 2015 *Nursing Informatics: Scope and Standards of Practice, Second Edition*, highlights genetics and genomics as new functional areas of NI practice, and explores new innovative roles in telehealth, analytics and consumer informatics. This new book will guide you through that evolution as it serves not only as a primer for nurses interested in NI, but also as a resource for other professionals in transition.

The healthcare environment is expanding its focus from patients to consumers, mainframes to mobile, data to intelligence, and paper-based to digital, and informatics nurses are at the forefront of these changes.

We invite you to start your NI education with this book, and join us on this exciting informatics journey!

Introduction

"Unless we are making progress in our nursing every year, every month, every week, take my word for it, we are going back."

—Florence Nightingale

In 1992, the American Nurses Association's Congress of Nursing Practice established nursing informatics (NI) as a specialty practice. In the 20+ years since its recognition, NI has spread and flourished, influencing every aspect of the U.S. healthcare landscape. Today, nurse informaticists can be found at the bedside, in information technology (IT), within the C-suite, and in government at the local and federal levels.

The scope and standards of this profession, updated every five years, have also grown in order to meet the opportunities—and challenges—of a healthcare landscape tectonically shifting while adjusting to the dizzying array of new technologies (and attendant regulations).

What is nursing informatics? Who are the people behind the specality? What careers can be—have been—forged from its practice?

This book is meant to provide some answers.

An Introduction to Nursing Informatics: Evolution & Innovation offers a concise history and current state of NI and serves as an introduction to the specialty's scope, influence, and growth within the healthcare industry.

Chapter 1 defines nursing informatics as a specialty, the different professional roles and titles being used, as well as the various reporting structures in operation today. Once this foundation is laid, **Chapter 2** builds a concise history of the profession, the pioneers and the key moments that led to the development of NI.

Chapter 3 provides a snapshot of NI today, including technologies, influential policies and a walk-through of the nurse informaticist's role in designing the electronic health record (EHR).

Chapter 4 looks into the future, the impact of emerging technologies on nursing and the importance of data visualizations. Look for clear takeaways and resources provided.

As many of you reading this book are new to nursing—even new to healthcare—it also serves as a roadmap to get your journey off on the right foot. As **Chapter 5** describes, the career opportunities for nurse informaticists are incredibly diverse—and continue to grow.

To help you, the reader, reflect upon the information provided in each chapter, there is a section in the Appendix of case profiles with questions listed by chapter. These profiles present concepts discussed in each chapter and are intended to stimulate discussion within the classroom or by study groups on the topics covered in the chapter. Individuals may also want to review the profiles to gain a broader comprehension of the material discussed in each chapter. We suggest that you take the time to review these questions for a better insight into the scope of NI.

This book is a great resource for students or those new to health IT, and can even serve as a reference guide for the many nurses currently working as informaticists.

CHAPTER 1

A Discipline Defined

Susan K. Newbold, PhD, RN-BC, FAAN, FHIMSS, CHTS-CP

Technology surrounds us in our personal and professional lives. The "Internet of Things" first mentioned by Ashton[1] in 1999 is described as a system in which the Internet is connected to the physical world by way of ubiquitous sensors. We are not yet to the point at which all data in healthcare is automated, but we are moving toward more automation in healthcare and other areas of our lives. Increasingly, our health records are being automated. Eventually, we will all have an electronic health record (EHR) that tracks our health, wellness, and illness from birth to death.

Many factors are leading us to utilize more health information technology (IT). In the U.S. healthcare system, there are issues with access to care, fragmentation of care, quality issues, and cost of care. Driving the use of technology are federal incentive programs to adopt and meaningfully use and standardize IT.

There are challenges to the adoption of health IT. Software products need to be more usable with better connections to other software. For example, not all environments have the ability to pass data from one healthcare site to another. When a patient moves from the hospital to a rehabilitation unit to the home, the information needed for patient care must move as well. Often our electronic records do not tell the "patient story," but consist of drop-down menus and click boxes. Finding the money to pay for new systems and measuring the value of those systems are additional challenges. Employing the right personnel to select, implement, and maintain systems is an issue as there are not enough people skilled in both healthcare and IT in the workforce.

In the midst of the explosion of technology in healthcare, the patient role is changing from one that is the recipient of care to one that is an engaged partner in his or her healthcare. Consumers of healthcare might use a personal health record (PHR), which is similar to an EHR, except that patients can control the data that go into it. Through the PHR, one can make appointments, request prescription refills, communicate with a healthcare provider, and pay bills. With some PHRs in use today, patients can input healthy practices such as tracking food intake, blood pressure, weight, and exercise.

DEFINITION OF HEALTHCARE & NURSING INFORMATICS

Healthcare informatics is defined by the Office of the National Coordinator for Health Information Technology (ONC) as "the application of information science and technology to acquire, process, organize, interpret, store, use, and communicate medical data in all of its forms in medical education, practice and research, patient care, and health management."[2] It is also known as *medical informatics*. There are many sub-areas of healthcare informatics, including nursing, dental, radiology, nutritional, veterinary, consumer, and health information management.

> Nursing informatics (NI) is a specialty that integrates nursing science with multiple information management and analytical sciences to identify, define, manage, and communicate data, information, knowledge, and wisdom in nursing practice. NI supports nurses, consumers, patients, the interprofessional healthcare team, and other stakeholders in their decision-making in all roles and settings to achieve desired outcomes. This support is accomplished through the use of information structures, information processes, and information technology.[3]

This is the most accepted definition of nursing informatics used in the United States, refined over time, and published by the American Nurses Association. Although this definition may seem complex, when dissected it makes sense.

Let us look at the first sentence, "Nursing informatics (NI) is a specialty that integrates nursing science with multiple information management and analytical sciences to identify, define, manage, and communicate data, information, knowledge, and wisdom in nursing practice."

Nurses work in a discipline that must integrate concepts from other fields in order to accomplish the work of providing safe, efficient, and effective care. Informatics and other nurses do not work in isolation, but need to partner for providing better care. In this definition, we see the continuum of data to information to knowledge to wisdom, which are concepts that increase in intricacy. To continue, nurses support all those who are associated with healthcare in all settings to make evidence-based decisions. In the next line, "information structures" refer to nursing and healthcare terminologies (CCC, NIC, NOC, NANDA, CPT, ICD-10, etc.). Information structures organize data, information, and knowledge for processing by computer systems. Information technology includes computer hardware, software, communication, and network technologies.

Not all nurses are informatics nurse specialists, but all nurses need to understand nursing informatics concepts. All nurses utilize data and put it together in meaningful ways to create information. The information then can contribute to the creation of new nursing knowledge. Health information systems are being integrated into every nursing role at the point of care and beyond. We are moving past the stage at which we merely input data to now understanding the information being created about the individual patient and patient populations.

A goal of nursing informatics is to support the "Triple Aim" of healthcare, which is improving the experience of care, improving the health of populations, and reducing per capita costs of healthcare.[4] Nurses who understand nursing and healthcare informatics are likely to help to improve the delivery and safety of patient care.

EVOLVING ROLES FOR NURSES

Some nurses think that informatics is a new field, but nurses have worked in this area for more than 40 years. In the early 1980s, a nurse who worked in the data processing department was typically called the "computer nurse." During that time, we implemented order entry and result-reporting systems (nursing systems were not well developed and widespread) and we trained other users on these systems. Some nurses developed information systems while working for a vendor organization or in the data processing department of a hospital.

Florence Nightingale is credited with being a statistician, collecting and using data to alter the way patients were cared for in the Crimean War. Perhaps she could be called the first informatics nurse because she used analytical methods to manipulate data to understand how to care for patients. We have come a long way as a profession and in using data and information to make informed decisions since the days of Ms. Nightingale.

THE EARLY ROLE OF THE NURSE
IN MEDICAL INFORMATICS

According to Hannah, Ball and Edwards,[5] the first MedInfo conference on medical informatics in Stockholm in 1974 included only five papers authored by nurses. One paper was written by Maureen Scholes, a registered nurse from England who is credited with coining the term "nursing informatics" in the early 1980s. Informatics was derived from the French word "informatique" referring to information. Scholes was instrumental in the hosting of the First International Conference on Nursing and Computing in 1982, held in the United Kingdom. The involvement of nurses in health IT has increased significantly since the early 1980s. In June 2016, the 13th International Congress on Nursing Informatics will be held in Geneva, Switzerland, with an expected attendance of more than 1,000 nurses from many countries.

The American Medical Informatics Association (AMIA) has a very active Nursing Informatics Working Group. One of their key projects has been to capture the history of pioneers in NI. These are nurses who have had an early and sustained contribution to the field of NI. The overall purpose of AMIA's Nursing Informatics History Project is to document and preserve the history of NI. Nurses are invited to listen to the words of our nursing leaders to learn how the profession has developed. There are three main components of this project:

- NI pioneers and nursing informatics organizations have been solicited to preserve their materials in an archive started by Dr. Virginia Saba at the National Library of Medicine in 1997.
- Stories of the pioneers in NI are being videotaped and made available through AMIA's website.
- Historical research has started which documents the evolution of informatics as a specialty in nursing.[6]

NURSING SPECIALTY PRACTICE

Although nurses had been working with IT for many years, NI was formally recognized as a specialty in 1992 by the American Nurses Association. Nursing research regarding NI is increasing and there is a cadre of nurses who identify themselves as informatics nurses. Nurses are employed as informatics nurses, speak at conferences, write books and papers, create journals, participate in professional organizations, take courses at the university level, seek certification, and conduct research.

The Healthcare Information and Management Systems Society (HIMSS) is a membership organization (and publisher of this book) that provides tremendous support for nurses interested in informatics.[7] Surveys, webinars, the HIMSS *Online Journal of Nursing Informatics*, nursing informatics books, blogs, and the Annual HIMSS Conference & Exhibition are among the plethora of offerings. HIMSS' student rate encourages membership by those new to the field or interested in healthcare informatics.

JOB TITLES FOR INFORMATICS NURSES

The American Nurses Association's *Nursing Informatics: Scope and Standards of Practice, Second Edition*[3] defines two titles for nurses working in informatics—the informatics nurse and the informatics nurse specialist. The informatics nurse (IN) is a registered nurse with an interest or experience in an informatics field, such as nursing informatics. The informatics nurse specialist (INS) is a registered nurse with formal graduate level education in informatics or a related field. Although the ANA recommends use of these two titles, there are actually a couple thousand titles in use for nurses working within informatics. This makes it difficult to understand who is actually working in informatics and to do any comparison of job titles for purposes of evaluation and salary, etc.

In a study of the top titles used by nurses identifying with the informatics field in this author's database, there were 6,211 unique titles used out of 23,667 nurses.[8] The number of instances of use is indicated followed by the title in **Table 1-1**. *Clinical Analyst* was the most often used informatics title in the database. The recommended title of *Informatics Nurse Specialist* was used by only 35 nurses and *Informatics Nurse* was not on the list of the top 31 titles. Perhaps nurses should think about moving to a more finite number of titles and use the recommended two titles to be able to more clearly define who they are and compare job duties and salary, etc.

Table 1-1: Top Titles Used by Nurses in Informatics—2013.

Number of Nurses	Title
236	Registered Nurse (or title not specified)
220	Clinical Analyst
219	Informatics Nurse
154	Consultant
133	Clinical Informatics Specialist
132	Assistant Professor
130	Graduate Student Nursing Informatics
125	Clinical Systems Analyst
117	Associate Professor
90	Nursing Informatics Specialist
84	President
82	Clinical Informatics Analyst
82	Project Manager
75	Director
73	Senior Consultant
70	Professor

Table 1-1: Top Titles Used by Nurses in Informatics—2013. (cont.)

Number of Nurses	Title
67	Clinical Informatics Coordinator
62	Senior Clinical Analyst
59	Systems Analyst
58	Clinical Informaticist
58	Manager
52	Nursing Informatics Coordinator
51	Nurse Informaticist
50	Clinical Informatics
49	Nurse Manager
47	Clinical Informatics Nurse
46	Clinical Consultant
45	Director, Clinical Informatics
42	Senior Systems Analyst
35	Informatics Nurse Specialist
35	Chief Nursing Officer

It is easy to confuse *roles* with *titles*. The list below presents the functional areas of NI described in *Nursing Informatics: Scope and Standards of Practice, Second Edition*.[3] Those working in informatics would not be serving in all areas, but would focus on one or more functional areas combined within a particular NI position.

- Administration, leadership, and management.
- Systems analysis and design.
- Compliance and integrity management.
- Consultation.
- Coordination, facilitation, and integration.
- Development.
- Educational and professional development.
- Genetics and genomics.
- Information management/operational architecture.
- Policy development and advocacy.
- Quality and performance improvement.
- Research and evaluation.
- Safety and security.

A ROLE FOR EVERY NURSE

Not all nurses care to be informatics nurses or informatics nurse specialists. Yet every nurse does have a role in informatics. According to the *Scope and Standards,* "Nurses are skilled in managing and communicating information and are always concerned with content quality." [3]

We can use health IT to help manage and communicate information. The typical nurse will have a specialty area such as perioperative nursing as a central focus and then use the concepts of data, information, knowledge, and wisdom to provide effective healthcare delivery regardless of where he or she works. All nurses can use their knowledge of workflow, skill sets, and clinical experience to identify where improvements are needed and can be improved through the use of IT.

Within a short time, informatics will be more entrenched in our educational programs and in practice and will be more accepted as a component of our role. The nurse may focus on using information applications and technology, whereas the informatics nurse may focus on the design, development, implementation, and evaluation of applications and technologies, ensuring their safety, quality, effectiveness, efficiency, and usability.[3]

REPORTING STRUCTURES

In 2014, HIMSS conducted a survey of 1,047 informatics nurses and found that 71 percent of respondents worked in a hospital or corporate offices of a healthcare system. Of those respondents, more than half (53 percent) stated they report to the information systems (IS) or IT department.[9] Thirty percent reported to the nursing department, which was slightly less than two previous survey years. Twenty-one percent reported to administration. As the figures total more than 100 percent, it is assumed that several of those surveyed reported to more than one department (see **Figure 1-1**).

"Which department is the best for reporting?" is a common question. There is no easy answer, as there are pros and cons of reporting to IS/IT versus nursing. The culture of the organization may dictate which fit is best. For this author's entrance into informatics, it was best to report to IS/IT to learn the more technical side of informatics.

In other organizations, a strong nursing executive officer may be able to offer strong leadership.

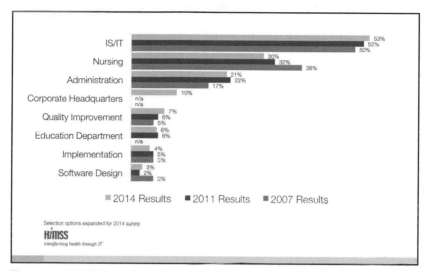

Figure 1-1: HIMSS 2014 Nursing Informatics Workforce Survey Reporting Structure for Informatics Nurses. (From the HIMSS 2014 Nursing Informatics Workforce Survey. Used with permission.)

SCOPE & STANDARDS OF NURSING INFORMATICS PRACTICE

Nursing Informatics: Scope and Standards of Practice[3] was first published in 1995 and 1996 as two separate documents (now combined as one). It has been revised over the years and is a must-read resource for defining the breadth and depth of the profession of informatics nursing. Importantly, it defines the informatics competencies for all nurses—not just informatics nurses.

The definition of NI was recently updated to include analytical sciences and stresses the interprofessional nature of the profession. This resource also addresses metastructures, concepts, and tools of NI, functional areas for NI, competencies, ethics, and the future of NI.

SUMMARY

This chapter provided an introduction to healthcare and NI. The purpose and goals of NI were defined. The different roles, available job titles and reporting structures were described along with the impact, pros and cons of each. This chapter also discussed the evolving scope and standards of the practice of NI. Every nurse has a role related to informatics, and understanding how to apply IT appropriately can help provide better patient care.

References

1. Ashton K. That 'internet of things' thing. *RFID Journal*. Jun 22, 2009. Accessed Jan. 30, 2015. Available at: www.rfidjournal.com/articles/view?4986.
2. U.S. Department of Health & Human Services. Office of the National Coordinator for Health Information Technology; 2014. www.healthit.gov. Accessed Jan 30, 2015.
3. *Nursing Informatics: Scope and Standards of Practice, Second Edition*. Silver Spring, MD: American Nurses Association; 2015.
4. Berwick DM, Nolan TW, Whittington J. The triple aim: care, health, and cost. *Health Affairs*. 2008;27(3):759-769; Doi 10.1377/hlthaff.27.3.759.
5. Hannah K, Ball M, Edwards M. *Introduction to Nursing Informatics, Third Edition*. New York: Springer; 2010.
6. AMIA Pioneers in Nursing Informatics History Project. Accessed Jan 30, 2015. Available at: www.amia.org/working-groups/nursing-informatics/history-project.
7. Healthcare Information and Management Systems Society (HIMSS). www.himss.org.
8. Newbold SK. Database of informatics nurses. 2014.
9. HIMSS 2014 Nursing Informatics Workforce Survey. HIMSS. Accessed Jan 30, 2015. Available at: www.himss.org/ni-workforce-survey.

CHAPTER 2

The Origins and Evolution of Nursing Informatics

By Sejal Patel, PhD; Grischa Metlay, PhD; Kathy Lesh, PhD, EdM, MS, RN-BC; and Linda Fischetti, MS, RN

Just as the study of man leads us to look back to our evolutionary ancestors and the study of flight leads us to explore history well before the Wright brothers' first success at Kitty Hawk, the study of Nursing Informatics (NI) appropriately begins decades before the discipline was created. In the 1940s nurses were adopting classification, information management, and operations research methods to understand the science of nursing. Many of the nurses who were leading activities to quantify nursing outcomes, methods, resource models, and practices were the same nurses that quickly adopted computers to support this work. This early history of NI prior to its formalization as a specialty is important for fully appreciating NI's current accomplishments.

As this chapter shows, NI's early pioneers applied their professional expertise toward patient needs, hospital management, and information flows to improve systems geared toward healthcare planning and management. In addition to applying their expertise toward the design of these systems, early NI pioneers also used these tools to further the scientific basis of nursing care and improve the profession itself.

This chapter introduces some NI pioneers and describes their early engagement with computers and information systems, their efforts to organize and educate nurses with interests and experience in informatics, and their endeavors to enhance nursing research and practice more generally through standardizing nursing information and terminology systems.

This chapter divides the recent history of NI into three key periods. First, beginning in the 1940s, nurses allied with operations researchers and industrial engineers to adapt computers and information management to healthcare settings and practices. The next period, which began in the late 1970s, saw the development of standardized classification systems for nursing diagnoses, nursing interventions, and patient outcomes to advance the profession of nursing and improve patient care. The most recent period in the history of NI is characterized by the revolutionary use of technology in healthcare environments and the formalization of NI as a speciality within the nursing profession. This period is characterized by what many equate with NI today—the incorporation of nursing concepts into machine-readable health terminologies, the collaborative development of interprofessional informatics, and the expansion of research on the impacts of nursing on patient outcomes across the continuum of care.

THE ROOTS OF A NEW SPECIALTY: 1940–1980

Economic factors in the 1940s fundamentally changed care delivery environments. The increased availability of employer-based health insurance, the introduction of new inpatient technologies and services, and the influx of federal funding for hospitals following the Hospital Survey and Construction Act of 1946 had transformed hospitals from places for rest and convalescence into complex organizations with numerous departments, personnel categories, and payment streams.

This evolution led to an increased demand for managerial sense and logistical planning in healthcare settings, which in turn led to efforts across the country to identify approaches to rational health planning and hospital management that would help meet patient needs in a more efficient and effective manner.[1] These developments, in addition to concerns over healthcare worker shortages, particularly in nursing, and the rising cost of healthcare, popularized operations and systems thinking in the healthcare domain.

Beginning in the 1940s, nurses, along with operations researchers, industrial engineers, hospital administrators, and public health officials, among others, began embracing the notion that patient needs, although variable, could be identified quantitatively and that models based on patient classification schemes could be used to predict the resources required for patient care. Nurses began partnering with operations researchers and industrial engineers to adapt the approaches used in systems engineering to healthcare. During this period, public health officials began actively surveying community and regional health needs in an effort to adequately allocate public health personnel.[2] Together, these groups created and tested models for rational planning and management aimed at effectively distributing resources while maintaining healthcare quality.

Hospital Management Systems

From the start of these activities, nurses participated in interprofessional teams alongside operations researchers and industrial engineers to better understand and develop approaches to plan and manage healthcare resource use. As primary overseers of the flow of information about patients throughout the hospital setting, nurses became essential in efforts to capture and codify information flow within hospitals for modeling purposes.

For example, Rita Zielstorff, an NI pioneer, began her initial work in healthcare informatics when she responded to a posted newsletter soliciting nurses to help design an automated medication system in the Laboratory of Computer Science at the Massachusetts General Hospital. In that role, and in other subsequent positions involving the development of information systems, Zielstorff contributed her knowledge of nursing practice.

As she recalled, "It was because I was using my nursing expertise, my knowledge of how nurses particularly handled medications, and how they recorded medications, that I was hired to participate in the design of this automated medication system."[3]

Through using their insights into the operation of hospitals and other healthcare delivery institutions, nurses embraced an interprofessional approach, partnering in particular with operations researchers to develop patient classification systems that would effectively predict the resources required to treat a given population. Hospitals found that such systems more accurately predicted the amount of care required by various departments and services and thus, optimized overall patient care. Nurses also helped in these endeavors by dividing nursing procedures into a manageable number of tasks and by developing coefficients to represent cost in utility and salary for each. These early efforts resulted in staffing and time studies directed at improving the quality and quantity of nursing services. The interprofessional collaboration between nurses and operations researchers was critical to these early efforts. As one operations researcher remarked, "The nursing profession has taken commendable leadership in cooperating with efforts to analyze and improve patient care."[4]

Health Resource Planning

The 1960s saw historic economic influences on healthcare, with new federal legislation including the Medical Assistance to the Aged Act of 1960, the Community Health Services and Facilities Act of 1961, the Nurse Training Act of 1964, and the Social Security Amendments of 1965 authorizing Medicare and Medicaid, injecting millions of dollars into the American healthcare system. Sanctioning these expenditures was the country's growing expertise in accurately assessing and distributing healthcare resources. In addition, this period saw increasing requirements for reporting as well as sophistication in the approaches used to assess and analyze health worker resources throughout the country.

Once again, nurses played an early and critical role in developing the models and approaches used in health labor resource models. Nurses in the United States Public Health Service (USPHS) had been producing nurse manpower analyses on community nursing since 1937. To produce these analyses, nurses not only surveyed the number of community nurses across the country, but also sought information about the specific needs of the communities served.

As Virginia Saba, an NI pioneer, explained, the flow of information "starts with the nurse, who collects data as she provides service to the patient. The data are then transferred to the reporting system, where they can be translated into information of significant value to all components of the agency and all levels of personnel."[5]

By 1972, when Saba took the lead in preparing these surveys, the models had expanded from providing basic descriptive statistics on nurses working in community settings to relating nursing personnel and nursing programs to the total public health resources of the community. This expanded focus facilitated the measurement of relationships between services offered by public health agencies, personnel providing the services, and characteristics of the population serviced. It also provided a better statistical base for projecting nurse manpower needs in public health, out-of-institution, and community nursing services. As with hospital management systems, health resource planning required accurate predictions of the resources required to meet healthcare needs—activities toward which nurses, like Saba, contributed greatly.

Nurses and the Application of Computers

Nurses like Saba and Zielstorff who had already been leading the study and quantification of nursing practices were early adopters of computers in healthcare settings. For example, they influenced the early development of hospital management systems and became leaders in adopting information management systems in their respective institutions.

At the USPHS, the use of computers became almost inevitable as its community nursing surveys grew more sophisticated. Assistant Surgeon General Rear Admiral Jessie Scott wrote in the foreword to *Management Information Systems for Public Health/Community Health Agencies*, "With the increasing cost of health manpower and the multiplying complexities in the delivery of healthcare, it is no longer possible to plan and predict the manpower needs and staffing requirements of public health/community nursing agencies without computer assistance."[6]

These needs prompted the USPHS, specifically its Division of Nursing, which was led by Scott, to fund early initiatives focused on the use of computers and information systems in nursing. As a result, key players with backgrounds in manpower analyses, like Saba, went on to develop management information systems for other public health/community health agencies.

Nurses also played central roles in overseeing the implementation of information and management systems in healthcare settings. For example, Carol Romano, who designed and implemented one of the first computerized medical information systems in 1976 and established the first graduate curriculum in nursing informatics, led the development of interfaces between the various management information systems used in different hospital departments. According to Romano:

> As one looks at all of the different types of clinical systems that are used in a healthcare environment, it becomes important to understand how the interfaces of these systems need to work. For example, a nutrition system is important, but it needs to connect with the diet order, and then how the nurse communicates electronically to let the dietary system know when the patient is NPO, a medical term for "nothing by mouth" or when diet trays have to be served, and whether diet drug allergies are integrated into the clinical systems.[7]

Nurses detailed the clinical and operational needs for the proper flow of information from one department to another. Romano remarked, "Nurses have always been in a critical position to handle information and to integrate it across the discipline."[8] Like Romano, nurses across the country played similar roles in ensuring the proper integration of information systems in healthcare settings.

ESTABLISHING A NEW SPECIALTY
NI IN THE 1980s–1990s

The nurses who took on the responsibility of managing these systems became self-taught users, often enrolling in computer and programming courses as needed to support their ability to better use and develop these systems and the information they produced. Nurse administrators quickly saw the need to promote the inclusion of nurse informaticists in decisions about which information systems to adopt, in large part to assist their own evaluation of staffing needs and workflows.

As a chief nurse at the NIH Clinical Center told Romano, "We're going to let the technology people worry about the technology, and we're going to worry about what it is about nursing care that the system can do for us, and what is the information piece for our nursing care process that we want to capitalize on."[9]

However, in the early 1980s, these nurses were often making such systems decisions independently—without leadership, without organization, without standards. Without realizing it, nurses were creating the basis of a new professional specialty they would later refer to as nursing informatics. However, this transition required a great deal of collaboration, convening, and sharing of ideas to create a common foundation. Through conferences, educational programs, and leadership roles in major nursing organizations, NI pioneers like Zielstorff, Saba, and Romano communicated the role of nurses in information systems, the demand for this expertise, the need for further training, and how the nursing profession as a whole would benefit from the contributions of NI.

Conferences

Early conferences on computers and nursing played a critical role in bringing together nurses who had worked on hospital information and management systems and were eager to develop their skills in and knowledge of this area. Motivating NI pioneers like Saba and Romano to organize such conferences were the questions they and a handful of other nurses had about operating and maintaining these systems.

Saba, who convened a nursing session at the Symposium on Computer Applications in Medical Care (SCAMC) in 1977, found a large number of receptive attendees eager to build their knowledge and networks. In 1981, Romano sent out flyers for a conference titled *Computer Technology and Nursing* at the NIH. The experience was eye opening for Romano. For one, she received a far greater number of responses than she had originally expected.

As she explained, "We thought we would get maybe a hundred people...and we were shocked to get a thousand people come to the conference."[10] The event was also surprising because it brought to the fore the collective need for information sharing and collaboration in this area. For many attendees, this was their first interaction with other nurses working with computers and on classifying activities for health information, and many were eager for answers to questions and to acquire needed information.

The high turnout at these early conferences led to regular opportunities for nurses interested in computers and informatics to build their knowledge and networks. Saba's nursing sessions at SCAMC became an annual event; Romano went on to organize six more *Computer Technology and Nursing* conferences within the decade. Such forums were essential for building a network of nurses willing to collaborate on topics related to NI. Saba made a point of collecting contact information on all nurses who attended the SCAMC sessions and would send them regular updates on new initiatives, sessions, and conferences focusing on computers in nursing.

NI pioneers also used conferences to establish interest groups, like the Computers in Nursing interest group at SCAMC and working groups such as the International Medical Informatics Association's Working Group 8 on Nursing Informatics, which further served to build an emerging network of, and professional base for, nurse informaticists. Conferences also gave NI pioneers the opportunity to publish conference proceedings and special conference issues, as the journal *Computers in Nursing* began doing in 1984. Overall, conferences were instrumental in bringing to the attention of the nursing profession the growing interest, existing potential, and future contributions of the emerging speciality of NI.

Educational Programs

In the early 1980s, a spattering of workshops and seminars were available for providing nurses with a basic introduction to using computers in healthcare settings. For example, the University of Akron School of Nursing started holding an annual one-week workshop, beginning in 1980, called "Computer Usage in Healthcare" that introduced nurses to all aspects of computer applications in their field. Supporting these programs were the early books and textbooks published about nursing informatics during this period. Zielstorff's *Computers in Nursing*, published in 1980, was the first book on nursing informatics.[11] This was followed later in 1980 by *Nursing Information Systems*, edited by Harriet H. Werley and Margaret R. Grier.[12]

Nursing programs soon began offering undergraduate courses in nursing informatics as well. For example, in 1985 Saba led Georgetown University's School of Nursing elective NI courses in both its undergraduate and graduate programs. Marion Ball, not a nurse herself but a longstanding nurse advocate, along with Romano and Barbara Heller, Dean of the School of Nursing, spearheaded the effort to establish the first graduate degree in Nursing Informatics at the University of Maryland in 1988—a program responsible for producing the vast majority of nurse informaticists that joined the workforce in the 1990s.[13] These programs helped establish an NI workforce and enabled an even greater number of hospitals and other healthcare institutions to benefit from the work of nurse informaticists.

Nursing Organizations

Major nursing organizations supported the formalization of NI through providing platforms on which to build leadership and formalize classification systems, educational programs, and other aspects of NI. At the initiative of Saba and others, the American Nurses Association (ANA) launched the Council on Computers Applications in Nursing (CCAN), which allowed early NI pioneers to develop nursing information systems (NISs). The National League for Nursing (NLN) also formally supported NI through forming the National Forum of Computers in Healthcare in 1985, which became the Council on Nursing Informatics in 1989.

Through these councils, NI pioneers were able to pass national resolutions about the future of this emerging field. For example, the ANA and NLN approved resolutions urging nurse informaticists to assume leadership in the development of NISs and to include computer courses in educational programs, respectively. In 1982 the ANA created the Steering Committee on Classification of Nursing Practice (later named the Steering Committee on Databases to Support Clinical Nursing Practice and then the Committee for Nursing Practice Information Infrastructure) for the purpose of recognizing classification systems on ANA's behalf. This was an important function, because ANA-recognized classification systems later became part of the National Library of Medicine's Unified Medical Language System (UMLS®).[14] In 1984, the ANA created a Council on Computer Applications in Nursing to promote and oversee education on the topic.

NI as a Nursing Specialty

While the 1980s were notable for the growing recognition of NI through conferences, publications, educational programs, and formal and informal networks across the country, nurses engaged with computers, information processing, and analyses had little sense of belonging to a distinct specialty within nursing. Indeed, the definition of NI was limited to that of an activity based on skills and scope of practice for nurses in IT.

As one observer noted, during the 1980s, technology often defined the area of nursing informatics, with textbooks describing NI as any use of IT by nurses in relation to the care of their patients, the administration of healthcare facilities, or the educational preparation of individuals to practice the discipline.[15]

In other words, the impact of NI on the nursing profession as a whole was less recognized and appreciated. What helped NI establish itself as a speciality within nursing was its ability to articulate its role in promoting the profession of nursing, establishing a well-defined research and educational agenda, and eventually, building an accepted mechanism through which nurses could become credentialed in NI.[16]

Helping NI assert its place within the nursing profession as a whole was the seminal 1989 article by Judith Graves and Sheila Corcoran titled, "The Study of Nursing Informatics." Rather than describing NI as a set of skills, Graves and Corcoran described NI as a "combination of computer science, information science *and nursing science* [italics added] designed to assist in the management and processing of nursing data, information and knowledge to support the practice of nursing and the delivery of nursing care."[17] By emphasizing nursing science as a critical component of the work performed by nurse informaticists, they elevated the status of nursing informatics from a set of practices into a specialty in its own right. The article helped articulate a research and educational agenda for the new field as well—one in which NI enabled and supported improvements in the practice and delivery of nursing care.

With this clearly articulated role in the nursing profession, ANA recognized Nursing Informatics as a specialty practice in 1992. Steps towards certification began soon after, with ANA publishing the NI Scope of Practice statement and *Nursing Informatics: Scope and Standards of Practice* in 1994. Formal certification by the American Nurses Association Credentialing Center (ANCC) began in 1995.[18] Today there are more than 1,000 certified nurse informaticists, while thousands more have received graduate-level degrees and/or work in the practice of NI without certification.[19]

STANDARDIZING NURSING INFORMATION 1980–1995

Expanding, refining, and standardizing nursing information became a major focus of NI during the 1980s and 1990s. For example, when the ANA originally explored the development and testing of a classification system for use in all areas of nursing practice in 1986, the system, known as the North American Nursing Diagnosis Association (NANDA) Taxonomy I grouped "human responses to actual or potential health problems" according to nine response patterns. By the time ANA officially recognized the NANDA Taxonomy in 1992, it contained more than 100 nursing diagnosis labels.[20]

Driving NI's focus on classification systems during this period were efforts to strengthen the nursing profession as a whole. With an established professional base united by educational programs and national organizations, first- and second-generation NI pioneers began asking how NI could elevate the status of nurses while improving patient care.

At the beginning of the 1980s, a small cohort of nurses coalesced around the idea that the nursing knowledge base could advance if nurses collected standardized information about their activities and their patients. Each of these pioneers had seen the status of the nursing profession improve during the 1970s. They also felt strongly that continued improvements could only be assured if nurses were able to document their contributions to patient care and develop a solid foundation of objective nursing knowledge that could drive future improvements in clinical practice and health policy. These pioneers dismissed as unscientific the nursing theories that guided the profession during the first half of the 20th century. In their view, nursing interventions should not be defined as a residual category of "things that doctors don't do."[21]

Interventions needed to be precisely delineated, and they needed to be associated with patient outcomes in order to generate scientific evidence of their efficacy. The key to accomplishing these goals was in refining the documentation of nursing diagnoses and practices, as well as their impact on patient outcomes. As Norma Lang famously quipped, "If you don't name nursing you can't practice it, you can't teach it, you can't pay for it, [and] you can't put it in public policy."[22]

Joined by a common vision for nursing, these pioneers came together at conferences and *ad hoc* workshops to discuss how to construct standardized terminologies. This effort was motivated by the recognition that, as Margaret Grier argued at a 1977 conference, "problems arise in making nursing decisions because of difficulty in acquiring and processing information."

For Grier, nursing information was critical to proper clinical decision making, not to mention nursing education and research. To further these ends, it was necessary to design and develop "systems of information for nursing practice."[23] At that same conference, Werley stressed recent improvements in computing; she also emphasized to her colleagues the importance of ensuring that nurses played an active role in the creation of nursing information systems.[24]

External factors also contributed to the emphasis on expanding, refining, and standardizing nursing information during the 1980s. Early in that decade, Medicare introduced prospective payment systems and diagnosis-related groups and Congress passed legislation that provided strong incentives to form health maintenance organizations—all of which were intended to curb spiraling healthcare costs. As the federal government and other insurers sought to rein in costs, healthcare administrators became more cognizant of resource utilization. In such an environment, focused as strongly as it was on cost-cutting efforts, the ability for nurses to document their contributions and account for their activities became more important.

For example, since nursing costs were (and still are) factored into the room costs for an inpatient hospital stay, the documentation of nursing activities helped ensure that hospital administrators would not inappropriately eliminate nursing shifts to reduce overhead. The imperative to cut healthcare costs highlighted the need to more systematically document nursing's unique contributions to patient care, which in turn provided the incentive to standardize nursing terminologies in the 1980s.

NANDA Taxonomy, Omaha System, Nursing Minimum Data Set

The first major effort to classify nursing information began in 1973, when Kristine Gebbie and Mary Ann Lavin convened what they called the First Task Force to Name and Classify Nursing Diagnoses, which eventually led to the creation of the NANDA alphabetical list of nursing diagnoses. Nurse informaticists then worked to restructure NANDA's list of nursing diagnoses into a hierarchical taxonomy in preparation for submission to the World Health Organization for consideration for inclusion in the 10th revision of the International Classification of Diseases (ICD).[25]

At roughly the same time, staff and administrators at the Omaha Visiting Nurse Association set to work on their own classification system for public health nursing. Led by Karen Martin, these nurses believed that such a system would expedite staffing and care delivery while promoting professional autonomy and accountability. More comprehensive than the NANDA Taxonomy, the Omaha System encompassed interventions and an outcome scale as well as the types of client problems that the NANDA Taxonomy covered.

Beginning with a list of 49 nursing conditions in 1976, the Omaha System was expanded in 1986 to include 44 client problems, 663 interventions, and an outcome scale denoting relative improvement and decline. In 1992, the system was further refined, and that same year ANA recognized it as an official classification system.[26]

Work on the Nursing Minimum Data Set (NMDS), another nursing classification system, traces back to conversations between Harriet Werley and other participants of the 1977 Nursing Information Systems Conference. In the early 1980s, while working at the University of Wisconsin-Milwaukee School of Nursing, Werley approached Norman Lang, Dean of the School of Nursing, about developing a minimum data set for nursing information.

At the time, the U.S. Department of Health & Human Services was promoting the notion of a minimum health data set for collecting essential information about certain aspects of a healthcare system. Lang discussed the subject with other faculty at the nursing school and in 1985 the school hosted a three-day invitational conference, the outcome of which was the NMDS.

In 1990, the ANA recommended that the NMDS be used as the essential minimum data set for nursing information in any electronic patient record system. By 1994, the NMDS included 16 items, which consisted of elements covering nursing care (i.e., nursing diagnosis, nursing intervention, nursing outcome, and intensity of nursing care) as well as other items encompassing patient characteristics and administrative information.[27]

Nursing Intervention Classification (NIC) and Nursing Outcomes Classification (NOC)

Joanne McCloskey and Gloria Bulechek from the University of Iowa conducted other important work in nursing terminology classification. McCloskey and Bulechek became interested in systematizing nursing interventions in 1982 when they were teaching a graduate course on adult health nursing. This collaboration led to the publication of an award-winning textbook, *Nursing Interventions: Treatments for Nursing Diagnoses,* in 1985.[28] Their work piqued the interest of other faculty at Iowa for offering a robust, integrated classification scheme for interventions and outcomes. After the 1986 NANDA conference, McCloskey and Bulechek decided to mount a substantial effort to promote their approach.

Guided in large measure by the idea that clinical decision making required knowledge about nursing diagnoses, nursing interventions, and patient outcomes, McCloskey and Bulechek formed a research team in 1987, and in 1990 they received a three-year grant from the NIH to further develop their system. The Iowa research team completed the first version of the Nursing Intervention Classification (NIC) in 1992, which consisted of 433 interventions. Each intervention included a list of activities falling under the scope of that intervention.

The Iowa team developed a text, published in 1992, stating, "When nurses systematically use a common standardized language to document the diagnoses of their patients, the treatments performed, and the resulting patient outcomes, then we will be able to determine which nursing interventions work best for a given population."[29] In 1992, the Iowa team, led by Sue Moorhead, expanded their efforts to include an analogous classification scheme for patient outcomes, the Nursing Outcomes Classification (NOC). Like other classification initiatives, the motivation driving NIC and NOC revolved around demonstrating the impact of nursing practice on patient outcomes. Recognizing the sophistication of the NIC and NOC schemes, ANA officially recognized NIC in 1992 and NOC in 1997. The fourth edition of the NOC was published in 2008 and includes 385 outcomes.[30]

Entrenching Classification Systems and Researching Nursing Impacts: 1995–Present

Once nurse informaticists had standardized nursing terminologies, they turned to the task of integrating nursing classification systems and concepts into larger standardized health terminologies. Prompting this shift were new federal initiatives beginning in the 1980s that promoted the computerization of such terminologies. For example, in 1986, Congress funded the National Library of Medicine (NLM) to build the Unified Medical Language System (UMLS®), which provided health professionals and researchers with a centralized system to "build or enhance systems that create, process, retrieve, and integrate biomedical and health data and information."[31] Including nursing classification systems into these initatives was critical to ensuring nursing-relevant data were collected in new computer systems and available for nursing research and quality improvement needs.

Incorporating Nursing Concepts into Computerized Health Terminologies

Nurse informaticists worked to ensure that ANA-recognized systems were included in the UMLS® Metathesaurus, the first edition of which was released in 1990 and has since undergone several subsequent revisions. Starting in the mid-1990s, nurse informaticists at the ANA sent NLM the NANDA Taxonomy, Home Health Care Classification (HHC), an early version of NIC, and the Omaha System. As a result of these efforts, the NANDA Taxonomy, HHC, and NIC were incorporated into the UMLS® Metathesaurus in 1995, and the Omaha System was added in 1996.[32] Nurse informaticists also subsequently added and periodically updated other nursing terminologies for new versions of the UMLS® Metathesaurus.

Later in the 1990s, nurse informaticists also began integrating nursing concepts into the Systemized Nomenclature of Medicine Reference Terminology (SNOMED RT®), a comprehensive system of machine-readable clinical concepts. In 1998, nurse informaticists collaborated with the College of American Pathologists (CAP), the organization contracted to work with the United Kingdom's (UK) National Health Service to converge SNOMED RT and the UK's Clinical Terms Version 3 to create SNOMED Clinical Terms (CT), in large part to demonstrate that nursing concepts could be integrated into a machine-readable terminology system such as SNOMED CT.[33] For example, in a seminal article published in 1998, Suzanne Bakken and colleagues showed that nursing diagnoses contained in the NANDA Taxonomy and Omaha System could be disassociated into existing semantic linking systems. They further demonstrated that the resulting linked diagnoses were compatible with the semantic linking system in SNOMED CT.[34] Having produced this proof of concept, Bakken's team undertook further work to construct the semantic linkages needed to fully integrate the NANDA Taxonomy and Omaha System into SNOMED CT.

At the end of the 1990s and as part of the standardization of health concepts and the incorporation of nursing concepts into machine readable terminologies, nurse informaticists also moved to standardize the definitions of and distinctions between different types of concept groupings. The ANA acknowledged that not all groupings of nursing concepts were classifications and that different recognition criteria were needed for different types of concept groupings. ANA adopted definitions from the International Organization for Standardization (ISO) for terms such as classification, taxonomy, and terminology and broadened the scope of ANA recognition from nursing classification systems to terminologies that support nursing practice.

As other nursing concepts were subsequently added to the UMLS® Metathesaurus, the process of integrating new concepts was simplified in the early 2000s when nursing terminologies incorporated in the UMLS® Metathesaurus were routinely extracted into new editions of SNOMED CT.[35] Currently, SNOMED CT's Nursing Problem List subset contains 417 concepts which are included in the UMLS® Metathesaurus. Full integration of nursing concepts within SNOMED CT was a critical accomplishment for nurse informaticists because EHR vendors must use SNOMED CT to become certified and meet certain EHR Incentive Program requirements. As a result, it is now possible to collect standardized nursing data from multiple sources, an achievement that will facilitate further research on the impact of nursing on clinical outcomes.

Using Nursing Informatics to Support Quality Improvement Efforts

Developments in the U.S. healthcare system provided further impetus to conduct research on how nursing impacts patient outcomes. Growing dissatisfaction with cost-cutting in the mid-1990s created a backlash against managed care. In the aftermath of the failed Clinton healthcare reform initiative, insurers and employers searched for ways to increase access without the costs associated with the traditional fee-for-service system, or the restrictions on patient access associated with managed care. In this context, the notion of paying providers on the basis of quality—as opposed to volume (fee-for-service) or numbers of patients (managed care)—began to capture the attention of health policy makers.[36] Groups of employers and insurers launched initiatives like the Leapfrog Group and Bridges to Excellence to demonstrate the viability of "pay-for-performance" programs in the late 1990s and early 2000s. Medicare soon followed suit, launching its first value-based purchasing program, the End-Stage Renal Disease Quality Incentive Program, in 2010.

The growing value of research in this new context and the need to structure nursing's informatics-focused research agenda led to efforts to establish a firmer theoretical basis for NI. To give a few examples, Patricia Schwirian introduced model-driven research, rather than problem-driven research, based on four elements: information, user, context, and technology.[37] Carol Gassert, from the University of Maryland, added a fifth element—information processing.[38] Graves and Corcoran identified data, information, and knowledge as core to the definition of nursing informatics.[39]

In 1996, James Turley described a conceptual framework for NI based on the interaction between nursing science and informatics science, which included the fields of cognitive science, information science, and computer science.[40] Also in 1996, William Goossen, from the Netherlands, extended Graves and Corcoran's framework described earlier by including the processes of collecting, aggregating, representing, and using information and the nursing activities of decisions, actions, and evaluation.[41]

These models of nursing informatics have evolved from nursing and other sciences to provide the unique perspective in which nurse informaticists approach practice and research. A quick review of the published literature in NI over the past decade and a half reveals much activity across the different facets of these models, from the use of technologies, workforce competencies, education within specialty and traditional curriculums, information and terminologies, and efforts aimed at transforming the practice of nursing including work on evidence-based practice, quality, safety, and clinical decision support.

CONCLUSION

In 1863, Florence Nightingale noted the importance of information in improving healthcare. In her *Notes on a Hospital*, she wrote, "I have applied everywhere for information, but in scarcely an instance have I been able to obtain hospital records fit for any purpose of comparison."

Her efforts to correct this oversight highlighted the value in systematically collecting information on healthcare practices and outcomes and served as a critical turning point in healthcare generally, and the professionalization of nursing in particular. Nightingale recognized that information, collected systematically, was necessary to "show the subscribers how their money was being spent, what good was really being done with it, or whether the money was not doing mischief rather than good."[42]

Nurse informaticists have played a critical role in advancing Nightingale's noble mission. Through standardizing data collection on nursing practices and patient needs and outcomes and ensuring these standards are integrated into health information systems, they have enabled the profession of nursing to advance its knowledge base and secure its place in contemporary healthcare.

Nursing informatics can trace its roots to the 1940s, when the specialty's early pioneers began collaborating with operations researchers and industrial engineers to improve health planning and hospital management. The work of these early pioneers, which included systematically tracking information flows through hospitals and building models to accurately predict health resource needs, fit well with the needs of the computer systems that became more prominent in healthcare institutions from the 1970s on.

Recognizing the demand for more training and research in this area, NI pioneers began offering courses, writing textbooks, and organizing conferences that enabled the fledging area to become a bonafide nursing specialty. In the 1980s, nurse informaticists began more concerted initiatives to standardize classification systems and terminologies—efforts that helped ensure that nursing concepts, practices, and approaches were included in broader health information initiatives and acknowledged for their role in improving health outcomes more generally. Through entrenching classification systems and terminologies into intiatives like the UMLS® Metathesaurus, nurse informaticists ensured that technologies like electronic health records were standardized to capture information on nursing practices and patient outcomes—achievements that will ensure nursing's continued role in informing best practices and improving quality in healthcare.

REFERENCES

1. See, for example, Shuman LJ, Speas RD, and Young JP (eds.). Operations Research in Health Care: A Critical Analysis. Baltimore: Johns Hopkins University Press;1975.

2. Melhado E M. Health planning in the United States and the decline of public-interest policymaking, Milbank Quarterly. 2006; 84(2): 359-440.

3. Zielstorff R. (2008). Interview by AMIA Nursing Informatics Working Group, Nursing Informatics History Project, AMIA. Accesesed Aug 8, 2014. Available at: www.amia.org/sites/amia.org/files/Rita-Zielstorff-NIWG.pdf.

4. Levine E, Kahn HD. Health Manpower Models. in Shuman L; Speas RD; Young JP (eds.) Operations Research in Health Care. Baltimore: JHU Press; 1975: 338.

37. Schwirian PM. The NI pyramid—a model for research in nursing informatics. *Computers in Nursing.* 1986;4(3):134-136.
38. Gassert, C. A. Structured analysis: Methodology for developing a model for defining nursing information systems requirements. ANS Advances in Nursing Science. 1990; 13(2): 53-62.
39. Graves J.R. and Corcoran S. The Study of Nursing Informatics. Image: Journal of Nursing Scholarship. 1989; 21: 227-231.
40. Turley, J. P. Toward a model for nursing informatics. Image - The Journal of Nursing Scholarship. 1996; 28(4): 309-313.
41. Goossen, W. T. F. Nursing information management and processing: a framework and definition for systems analysis, design and evaluation. International Journal of Bio-Medical Computing. 1996;40(3):187-195.
42. Nightingale F. *Notes on Hospitals.* London: Longman, Green, Longman, Roberts, and Green; 1863. Accessed Aug 21, 2014. Available at: https://archive.org/details/notesonhospital01nighgoog.

CHAPTER 3

Nursing, Informatics, and Technology Today

By Kimberly Ellis Krakowski, MSN, RN, CAHIMS and Patricia Mook, MSN, RN, NEA-BC

Nursing informatics (NI) is the driving force for the evolution of healthcare today in the United States. This is propelled by the increasing use of health IT. The Institute of Medicine's report, *The Future of Nursing: Leading Change, Advancing Health*, acknowledged technology as a major contributor to increased patient safety and efficient and cost-effective care, and made profound recommendations for nurses to take a leadership role in transforming healthcare.[1] Clinical transformation will be based on technological advances that will require nurse informaticists to possess knowledge that was historically uncommon.

The nurse's role in the care of the patient has evolved, and with that has come a change in the way nurses think about and use technology to improve healthcare delivery. Every nurse today needs to be proficient in collecting and reviewing data and information related to their patients. The clinical practice requirements for nursing promote the development of skill sets important for informatics practice. The nursing process of assessment, problem identification, and care planning, combined with how nurses set priorities and always evaluate, prepare nurses to be early adopters and to employ and adapt the systems lifecycle approach for delivering informatics projects.

Project management—a vital skill in managing IT projects by establishing timelines, milestones, task dependencies, and resources—is more easily grasped by clinicians who have worked in areas of care requiring constant priority setting and evaluation, such as emergency or critical care.[2]

A nurse professionally trained in informatics is part of a greater discipline of healthcare informatics. These nurses know how to apply IT to enhance their clinical skills and work with nurses across the healthcare continuum to integrate the nursing science, computer technology, and information science resulting in improved communication, documentation, and efficiency. Possessing knowledge in these three areas positions nurse informaticists to lead the development of an emerging concept in healthcare—clinical intelligence (CI).

CI has risen out of the expansion of electronic data and is fueled by the prolific use of health IT. "Clinical intelligence" is defined as the electronic aggregate of accurate, relevant, and timely data into meaningful information and actionable knowledge in order to achieve optimal healthcare structures, processes and outcomes.[3] The rapid rate of change in medical knowledge is what is driving clinicians, particularly nurses, to use high-quality, well-aggregated, electronic clinical data to make sound decisions that will improve the quality, safety, and efficiency of the care delivered.

TODAY'S INFORMATICS NURSES

Nurses who practice informatics today still need to be grounded in utilizing the nursing process. Being experts in the practice of analytical and critical thinking makes informatics nurses ideal candidates to produce aggregated clinical data. In addition, their skills in understanding patient care delivery models and integration points for automated documentation give them a context to use this high-quality data to affect clinical outcomes.

The 2014 HIMSS Nursing Informatics Workforce Survey continues to suggest that the nurse informaticist plays a crucial role in the development, implementation and optimization of information systems and applications including clinical documentation, computerized provider order entry (CPOE) and electronic health records (EHR). Four times since 2004, HIMSS has surveyed members of the NI specialty to gain an understanding of the roles and responsibilities of the informatics nurse professional.

The 2014 survey findings help us understand many aspects about this field, but most importantly, the significance of this growing specialty (see **Figure 3-1**). The majority of the 1,047 nurse informaticists who participated in this research continues to work in a hospital setting—58 percent, increased from 48 percent in the 2011 survey, with another 13 percent working in corporate offices of a healthcare system, decreasing from 20 percent in 2011.[4] This increase of nurse informaticists in hospitals can be attributed to the pervasive technology changes evident in our hospitals and the need to possess knowledge that historically has not been common.

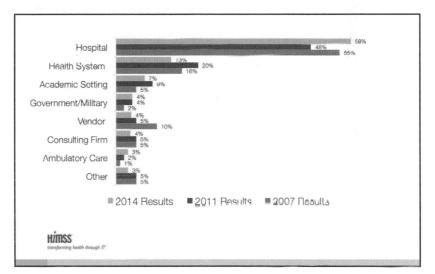

Figure 3-1: Growth of Nursing Informatics within the Healthcare Industry. (From the HIMSS 2014 Nursing Informatics Workforce Survey. Used with permission.)

While examining the nursing background of the nurse informaticist today, HIMSS found that close to 60 percent of respondents had a post-graduate degree, which includes a Master's Degree or PhD in nursing or related fields (see **Figure 3-2**).

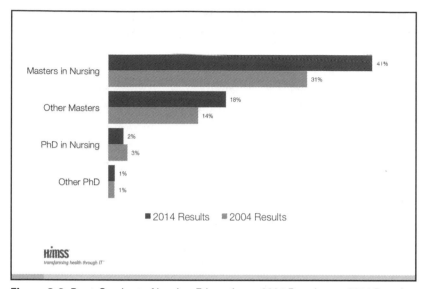

Figure 3-2: Post-Graduate Nursing Education—2004 Results vs. 2014 Results. (From the HIMSS 2014 Nursing Informatics Workforce Survey. Used with permission.)

When you look at the clinical experience of the respondents, 41 percent indicated more than 16 years of experience, down from 46 percent in 2011. Of note, the number of respondents reporting one to five years of clinical bedside experience increased from 12 percent in 2011, to 20 percent in 2014 (see **Figure 3-3**). An analysis of the training and informatics experience of the 2014 respondents shows that the percent of respondents who had obtained a post-graduate degree in nursing informatics or other informatics increased by 23 percent, from 21 percent in 2011 to 54 percent in the 2014 survey. When looking at the certification, we saw an increase of 3 percent to up to a total of 48 percent of all respondents, over the past three years.[4] (For the full results of the 2014 HIMSS Nursing Informatics Workforce Survey, visit www.himss.org/ni.)

TECHNOLOGY—TRANSFORMING WORKFLOW AND OUTCOMES

Many nurses are already savvy with technology despite the fact that, according to a 2013 survey conducted by the National Council of

State Boards of Nursing and the Forum of State Nursing Workforce Centers, 55 percent of the RN workforce is age 50 or older.[5]

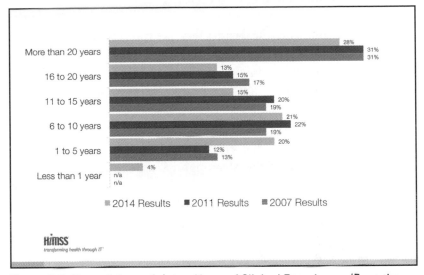

Figure 3-3: Nurse Informaticists—Years of Clinical Experience. (From the HIMSS 2014 Nursing Informatics Workforce Survey. Used with permission.)

Nurses, it is said, do not want to be passive consumers of technology.[6] Technology is what is driving transformational change and innovation in nursing care delivery models, and nurses are central to this transformation. With technology advances, we have the ability to accomplish regulatory work with standard practice, to provide efficiencies of space, and provide access to care resources resulting in improved safety and efficiency.

The Patient Safety and Quality Improvement Act of 2005 was implemented in response to growing concern about patient safety in the United States.[7] The goal of the act was to improve patient safety by encouraging voluntary and confidential reporting of events that adversely affect patients. The act highlights a focus on how patient safety event information is collected, developed, analyzed, and maintained.

This has driven the nurse informaticist to be a key contributor to the efforts of creating clinical documentation systems that will enable accurate collection of information. They are frequently leading clinical governance models in the role of a chief nursing information officer (CNIO), leading and guiding the work of design teams, analyst build teams, and testing teams as new EHRs are implemented.

The nurse informaticist's role clearly encompasses designing, building, and testing clinical systems. As we develop systems that are designed and built by clinical end-users like nurse informaticists, we will be better able to collect the patient safety event information that will assist healthcare organizations in identifying patterns of failures and proposing measures to eliminate patient safety risks and hazards.

Informatics nurses today work to assist in the development and training of technologies that enable us to better identify patients, which supports much of the Meaningful Use requirements that are guiding many initiatives being implemented in hospitals. Examples of this include bar-code medication administration, bar-code specimen collection, and the evolution and use of smart IV pumps.

Ultimately, one goal of NI leaders is to return more time at the bedside to nurses in order to provide safer care. Nurses are removed from tasks that are unnecessary with the development of lean process-transforming technologies. The development of systems that track time, awareness, supplies and people, by the mere ability to visualize improvements as a result of change, assists in reducing delays in care.

Nurse informaticists are leading value-stream analysis efforts to look for defects in workflow and clinical documentation to support organizational efforts to provide safer care. The ability to have clinical decision support at the point of care is also seen as improving safety. These efforts would include best practice alerts (BPAs) used to guide clinical practice. The nurse informaticist has knowledge of the technology and logic used to build these, and at the same time is able to understand the key areas in which clinical decision support will make a difference in the outcome of the patient's care.

Advances in communication technologies that direct and prioritize messages to facilitate quicker responses to patients and caregivers will also improve safety. Nurse informaticists are key in the assessment of workflows which are the core components needed in looking at process as EHRs are developed.

The Situation, Background, Assessment and Recommendation (SBAR) technique is one that is frequently used in healthcare as a communication technique:

- Situation: Describe the situation, patient, or question.
- Background: Highlight the important information, precautions, and issues.
- Assessment: Outline your read of the situation, problems, and precautions.
- Recommendation: State your recommendation, request, or plan.

Originally developed by the United States Navy as a communication technique that could be used on nuclear submarines, SBAR was introduced into healthcare in the late 1990s by Safer Healthcare as part of its Crew Resource Management (CRM) training curriculum. Since that time, SBAR has been adopted by hospitals and care facilities around the world as a simple yet effective way to standardize communication between caregivers.[8]

This tool is one that many nurse informaticists use in an expanded way, as a model to outline problems as they are identified in their work day. Using SBAR can help staff to problem solve, learn to respect each other's opinions by understanding why and how recommendations are drawn, and set a proactive approach that individualizes the corrective action that an organization may take to resolve a problem. The continued enhancement of technology tools will exponentially change how nurses plan, deliver, document, evaluate, and gather the evidence to provide safe, efficient care, and direct quality outcomes.

Healthcare environments frequently incorporate virtual office visits, online appointment scheduling and payment, mobile laboratories, and electronic medication prescribing. New technologies offer access and opportunities to provide quality care to patients in remote settings. Nurse informaticists become key in the role of not only developing these technologies, but also in the implementation of them in all settings, and in the creative work that goes into the marketing and communication developed to present to patients in our communities.

Training becomes an essential skill for many nurse informaticists. The development of mobile health technologies has grown tremendously and the need to teach patients how to use them has become a focus. The challenge for these technologies in healthcare is ensuring that the automated solutions completely interact with one another, as well as with the healthcare professionals and patients using them.[9]

While we still wait for conclusive research in the field of mobile health technologies for care provision, Shapiro–Mathews, a clinical nurse informatics specialist, and Barton encourage engaging patients and their families in mobile technologies using a modified patient engagement framework for the adoption of mobile health applications. This modified "Patient Engagement Framework" offers steps to the adoption of mobile health applications.[10] Their work clearly speaks to clinical nurse specialists as informaticists developing ways to improve patient engagement with mobile technologies.

Mobile and remote technology is an area in which nursing informaticists have just scratched the surface. The possibilities of how these technologies will impact care both for providers and patients are just beginning to be explored. The emergence of a unified mobile device strategy combining point-of-care documentation and multimodal communication is just now being realized. These solutions can support nursing practice in addition to assisting with the cognitive workload of nurses.

Advances in technology have enabled vendors to design products, based on smartphone technology, which allow flowsheet documentation into the EHR with bidirectional interfaces. In addition, data is enabled to flow back and forth between two software applications, bar-code medication administration, communication using voice over Internet protocol (VoIP), and secure text messaging. All this exists on a single device that can fit into a provider's pocket.

Many nurse informaticists are driving changes in practice based on their nursing research in these areas. Redding and Robinson (2009) saw that 31 percent of nursing interruptions occurred when another employee asked a nurse a question while both were face to face.[11] The Pew Research Center reported that as of January 2014, 90 percent of the adult population in the United States now owns a cell phone, and given that texting has become a standard form of communication, 81 percent of cell and smartphone users send and receive text messages, allowing nurses access to secure texting methods might reduce the number of face-to-face interruptions.[12]

Nurse informaticists provide the vision of a truly mobile clinical solution that enables practitioners to document their patient rounds as they are being done, see all assigned team members, place a call easily, and securely text other members of the care team. These are all possibilities, plus being able to choose the right mobile device that supports the cognitive workload of nurses by providing alerts—notifications that they see because they have the device at their fingertips in the moment. In addition, they allow access to the latest vital signs, medications, and pain scores with only a few taps of the finger.

Today's telecommunication choices have clinical ramifications beyond the purchase of a phone. Nurse informaticists need to be at the table during the evaluation and selection process. Utilizing technology to support the bedside clinician rather than causing barriers to safe practice is a goal that we all want to attain. Mobile technology is just one challenging area to which nursing informatics is contributing.

Much of this work is frequently conducted with a fast Plan-Do-Check-Act (PDCA) process that we are constantly trying to learn from and to create evidence to propell a flywheel to drive clinical transformation. As healthcare technology continues its rapid integration into so many aspects of care delivery, NI is at the forefront of providing the knowledge that nursing needs to lead change and advance health.

LEVERAGING NURSING KNOWLEDGE THROUGH LEGISLATION

In recent years, legislation has contributed to the growth of NI. Arguably, the spike occurred in 2009 when President Obama signed into law the American Recovery and Reinvestment Act (ARRA), which provisioned funding to promote health reform through IT adoption and implementation. This unprecedented decision allocated $19 billion to be allocated for "meaningful use" of EHRs in both the ambulatory and hospital settings.

Included in ARRA was the Health Information Technology for Economic and Clinical Health (HITECH) Act. This created the criteria for standards used to incentivize eligible professionals, facilities and critical access hospitals to use EHRs in a meaningful way.[11] The U.S. Department of Health & Human Services (HHS) developed the necessary objectives for achieving Meaningful Use (MU). Then the Centers for Medicare & Medicaid Services (CMS) established objectives for both eligible hospitals (EH) and eligible professionals (EP) to receive incentives.[12] MU is divided into five objectives and three stages.

The five MU objectives are to:
- Improve quality, safety, and efficiency and reduce health disparities.
- Engage patients and families.
- Improve care coordination.
- Improve population and public health.
- Ensure adequate privacy and security protections for personal health information.[12]

Stage 1 Meaningful Use focused on capturing healthcare information electronically in a coded format to monitor key clinical conditions and communicate information that supports overall care coordination.

Stage 2 Meaningful Use focuses on using health IT to impact and support continuous quality improvement at the point of care and includes the exchange of electronic health information.

Stage 3 Meaningful Use, set to begin in 2015, focuses on improvements in quality, safety and efficiency; decision support; patient self-management tools; and improving population health.[10] Health reform requires the ongoing advancement of health IT. But because technology cannot achieve success alone, innovative thought-leaders, like nurse informaticists, designers, implementers, and analytics experts will be essential.

In March 2010, the Patient Protection and Affordable Care Act (ACA), also known as Obamacare, offered hope in accomplishing legislation with the objective of providing both a decrease in healthcare expense and conversely an increase in quality patient care. This set the groundwork for not only providing access to healthcare for everyone, but also for promoting continuous improvement in healthcare so that patients may receive quality care.[13]

Health IT, inclusive of an optimized EHR and nurse informaticists, is essential for the ACA's success. Nursing has a unique body of knowledge that balances evidence-based practice, change management, process improvement and patient safety on a platform of nursing processes. These skills will be essential in improving health outcomes.

Nurses must be not only reactionary to the implementation of legislation, but also help in its creation. This can be done by actively participating in professional organizations. The Alliance of Nursing Informatics (ANI) is a collaborative of 25 organizations that speaks as a unified voice for nurses employed in practice, education, and industry.

In 2011, ANI stated that the use of standardized nursing and other health terminologies "is necessary and a prerequisite for decision support, discovery of disparities, outcomes reporting, improving performance, maintaining accurate lists of problems and medications, and the general use and reuse of information needed for quality, safety, and efficiency."[15]

Nurses should feel empowered to engage in conversation with political leaders, stating that policymakers depend on stakeholder input when making decisions about how to plan, implement, and enforce laws and regulations. The American Nursing Informatics Association (ANIA) remains committed to its specialty that integrates nursing science, computer science, and information science to manage and communicate data, information, knowledge and wisdom in nursing and informatics practice. This association identifies informatics practice as a specialty that is essential to the delivery of high-quality and cost-effective healthcare.[15]

HIMSS, mentioned earlier, is an additional resource to the entire informatics community. The recent 2014 HIMSS Nursing Informatics Workforce Survey showed a 158 percent increase in survey responses, which supports the premise that the nursing informatics workforce and interest in this area are growing at an accelerated rate.[4]

NI'S ROLE IN EHR DESIGN

As mentioned previously, MU requires the implementation of a certified EHR in the hospital and ambulatory settings, which is quite complex. Nurse informaticists play a significant role throughout the entire process, which starts with the executive leadership and board approving the capital investment in an EHR system.

The subsequent steps are typically inclusive of the request-for-proposal (RFP) process, vendor demonstration, end-user review or vendor fair, contract agreement, build-team creation, build-team training and certification, model system validation, design team identification, EHR design, EHR build, EHR testing, training curriculum development, subject-matter expert identification, end-user training, cut-over activities, implementation, optimization, and upgrade installation.

The vendor evaluation stage is when many nurses first enter the realm of informatics. As they review the selected EHR vendors, they are learning about EHR features, modules, applications and functionality. The input of nurses in selecting the EHR is extremely valuable because end user buy-in is essential in the success of the subsequent steps. And nurses typically make up 80 percent of the clinical workforce in any given hospital. Once the executive team has reviewed the top vendor candidates and selected the EHR for purchase, the team that will build the EHR and manage its implementation is identified. Bedside nurses, nurse clinical specialists, and nursing leaders are recruited for these positions because of their clinical expertise and relationships with the multi-disciplinary end-users.

When nurses have an interest in participating in the EHR build, but do not want to leave their positions at the bedside or administrative suite, they are perfect candidates for design teams. These individuals review the EHR's out-of-the-box functionality, then work to design the necessary functionality to provide evidence-based care or specialized treatment for unique patient populations.

Nurse managers and their staff are uniquely positioned to lead or join the effort to make a difference with nursing documentation and EHR design. Including the bedside nurse in the design is a way to make busy nurses aware that their documentation is used for other purposes.[16] Scherb, et al. believe it is the responsibility and obligation of nurses to ensure that clinical information systems are designed for the meaningful use of nursing clinical data.[17] Additional roles for nursing expose them to the informatics specialty, such as training.

Initially the training will be on how to document in the EHR, but later training will focus more carefully on workflow.

Go-live activities start hours before the new EHR system is turned on. Cut-over activities include entering current pertinent information into the new EHR for each patient. A combination of bedside nurses, build-team nurses, clinical nurse informaticists, and subject-matter experts will enter the required documentation so that it is there when the new EHR goes live.

For weeks after the initial implementation, nurses will continue to play a role. In fact, nurses will begin to realize that information technology is part of everything they do when providing care. Therefore, every nurse to some degree is a nurse informaticist.

Considering technology impacts the practice of nursing, every effort should be made to understand, implement, and optimize the technology available. Examples include best practice advisories, computerized order entry, multi-disciplinary plans of care, and standardized documentation templates.

Today's healthcare consumers demand a paradigm shift for how their care is communicated and provided to them. The patient is always at the center of what nurses do every day, in every moment, and with every touch. Nurses communicate through smartphone apps, video chat, and by monitoring electronic data via wearable devices. Nurses continuously strive to improve patient care and outcomes through the continuous analysis data now provided in the EHR. Nurses explore the newest technology and advocate that it be incorporated into their care of the patient to increase efficiencies of documenting and increase time spent directly with the patient. Nurses continuously seek opportunities to learn so that they may be thought leaders.

In the evolution of healthcare, nurse informaticists will continue to remain at the forefront.

References

1. Institute of Medicine (IOM). The Future of Nursing: Leading Change, Advancing Health. Washington, DC: National Academies Press; 2010.
2. Hassett M. Case study: factors in defining the nurse informatics specialist role. *Journal of Healthcare Information Management*. Spring 2006;20(2):30-35.

7. France
8. Canada
9. United States

The purpose of this chapter is to discuss those emerging technologies that, if leveraged appropriately, will serve as the technological accelerators for healthcare transformation. As you very well know, the transformation has already begun and is picking up speed. Your goal, then, is to understand not only the promise of these emerging technologies, but also their limitations so that they can be applied appropriately in the healthcare environment. Our clinical peers and our patients are counting on us as nurse informaticists to successfully implement and assist in the successful adoption of these new technologies. To do this you will have to be creative and innovative, and maintain a deep understanding of technologies available now, technologies on the near horizon, and technologies a few years out.

EMERGING TECHNOLOGIES

Human augmentation, quantum computing, volumetric and holographic displays, and wearables are just a few emerging technologies with which we as nurse informaticists must become familiar. In **Figure 4-1**, we see not only emerging technologies, but a projected trajectory of those technologies.

Every summer, Gartner publishes a report describing emerging technologies and places each on a hype curve that follows the pathway of a technology from innovation to mainstream productivity.[3] Once a new technology emerges, it then reaches a peak of inflated expectations at which the expectation of a technology exceeds the practical application of that technology.

We have all had an experience in which, before we had complete knowledge of a technology, we mentally applied it to a problem, only to find out later when we did have a more complete understanding of the technology, that it was not a fit for the problem we were trying to solve. This is why it is so important to fully understand technology before we apply it.

This leads to the next phase of the hype cycle: the "trough of disillusionment," in which our perceptions do not meet reality. Again, we can all think back to a technology implementation which we thought

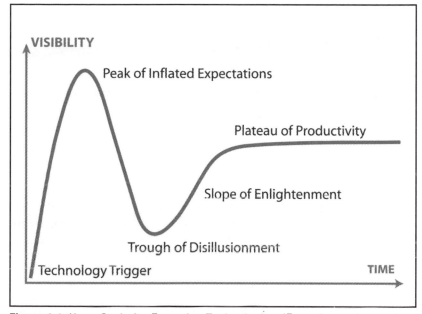

Figure 4-1: Hype Cycle for Emerging Technologies. (From Jeremykemp at en.wikipedia. Used with Permission.)[4]

was the ultimate technology solution, only to learn of unintended consequences reported back to us by users that forced us to go back to the drawing board to rethink our approach. Once a technology has made it past the trough of disillusionment, it begins a steady rise up the slope of enlightenment to the plateau of productivity, where the technology gains wide acceptance and is mainstreamed into practice.

Let us review some of the emerging technologies that are in the innovation trigger/peak of the inflated expectation phases and explore some of the ways they may be applied to healthcare. Remember, many of these will not be mature for several years, but it is important for us to be aware of them, follow them, and start to think of how we may apply them. We will not be able to cover all of the technologies, so make a list of your own and start to follow them as they mature. Make a note to check back with Gartner each summer to see how the various technologies are evolving and what new innovations have been triggered.

Wearables

Wearables are exactly what the name implies—technology that is worn on the body, such as a wristband—that collects and transmits data. Shipments of wearable devices are expected to grow to 250 million per year by 2018.[5] Some of the data collected presently by these devices includes heart rate, respirations, blood pressure, EKG, oxygen saturation, and activity.

Wearable devices are and will continue to be closely tied with the smartphone. They are comprised of various sensors that collect and transmit data to the smartphone, which then aggregates the collected data, sending it off to a cloud-based system that stores and interprets the data. In many cases, the smartphone also acts as a visualization layer, displaying the collected data and the analytics applied to the data.

Look for the bond between wearables and smartphones to become even stronger over the years. Future use cases include sensors to monitor epilepsy symptoms and blood glucose levels, and the expansion of wearables such as Google Glass into clinical practice. Also look for predictive analytics to enter the wearable space with the promise to predict events such as heart attacks before they occur. Wearable devices will be tied into population health strategies now that we are shifting focus to wellness. Wearable technology can help in the monitoring of the wellness level of a population. Think of the various use cases for this technology to monitor patients both inside and outside of the hospital. When reviewing use cases, think through adoption and ways to ensure the devices are used as intended.

Volumetric and Holographic Displays

Volumetric and holographic displays are still a few years out, but worth looking at now as there are some interesting healthcare use cases being discussed. For example, 3D images[6] will appear to float in volume and be easily manipulated. Bulky screens and projectors will not be needed, leading to greater mobility. Look for the first commercial products in 2016, with 3D images on smartphones in 2018.

Weaving Technology

Let us weave wearable technology with volumetric, holographic displays, and analytics that we will discuss in the next section together to solve a healthcare problem. The technology behind the solution may be a few years out, so keep in mind that this is a mental exercise to demonstrate tying technologies together.

Our patient is a 19-year-old male who was recently discharged from the hospital after his initial onset of Type 1 diabetes. Our patient has a wearable device that monitors vital signs, activity, diet, environment, and blood sugar. His smartphone is tightly coupled to his wearable device and features a volumetric and holographic display. The data from the wearable device is transmitted via the smartphone to an analytics platform to which algorithms are applied and notifications made to patients and care coaches when appropriate.

For the first two weeks our patient was doing great: he was eating well, taking his insulin, and receiving great feedback and encouragement from his "holographic" coach. During his third week he started to fall off his diet, despite coaching, resulting in an elevated blood-sugar state. The analytics platform monitoring our patient triggered an event in the population management system so that our patient's health coach could respond.

The health coach made a connection to the patient via his smartphone, assessed the situation and determined it best that our patient be seen in the diabetes clinic that day.

Albeit simple, these are the types of exercises you can do to tie various technologies together to solve healthcare problems. A white board session mapping out solutions is also very effective. Remember to include all stakeholders at some point in the process, and patients, too!

A MODERN HEALTHCARE ANALYTICS PLATFORM

With the advent of wearable devices, home monitoring devices, the Internet of Things and the data types listed below, there is a need for a platform to collect various data types and make sense of them all.

1. Electronic health records (EHR)
2. Pathology

3. Physiological monitors
4. Ventilator
5. Pharmacy
6. Real-time location service (RTLS)
7. Legacy data
8. Financial
9. Radiology
10. Laboratory
11. Social media
12. Home devices
13. Wearables
14. Omic data (data from interrelated fields, such as genomics and proteomics)
15. Medication administration
16. Clinical trials
17. Imaging
18. Bio repository
19. Open data
20. Internet of Things

The EHR, enterprise data warehouse, and existing analytics platforms are not ideally suited for the coming tsunami of healthcare-related data and the ever-increasing need to run analytics on that data. **Figure 4-2** details a modern healthcare analytics architecture that is capable of ingesting the data types listed above and future data types that are generated as outputs of emerging technologies. Please reference **Table 4-1** on pages 54 and 55 for a definition of terms that we will use for this discussion.

The EHR is not up to the task of complex pattern recognition, anomaly detection, machine learning, advanced algorithm development, and natural language processing. At this point you may be asking yourself: do I really need to know this? The answer is, yes, you do! The architects and developers of these systems will require subject-matter experts to get this right. Nurse informaticists were on the front lines of the configuration and implementation of the EHR, and now we need to be right in the thick of things during the build-out of analytics platforms. We know the data elements, their ontologies and their relationships, which data sources are authoritative and which

Table 4-1: Modern Healthcare Analytics Platform Terminology. (cont.)

Term	Description
High performance computing (HPC)	The use of supercomputers to rapidly solve complex problems.
In-memory	A database management system that stores data in memory, not on a disk, resulting in fast processing.
Internet of Things	Everyday devices connected to the Internet via sensors.
Machine learning	A process in which software learns during data processing and becomes more accurate over time.
MapReduce	The processes of breaking up problems into pieces that are then distributed across multiple computers on the same network or cluster.
Metadata	Data about data; information about stored data elements.
MongoDB	An open source reliable, high-performance, scalable document database.
Natural language processing (NLP)	Extracting information from text.
Neo4j	An open source graph database.
NoSQL	Databases that do not use the relational model, such as databases that store documents, tweets, and so on.
Ontology	A representation of a body of knowledge as a set of domain-specific concepts.
Open data	A data movement in which data sets are made available to the public for use without charge.
Open source	Applications in which the source code is available to the general public for use or modification.
Pattern recognition	Identification of patterns in data via algorithms.
Pig	A programing language used in the Hadoop framework.
Predictive analytics	The use of existing data sets and algorithms to predict the probability that a future event will occur.
Quantified self	A movement to incorporate data acquisition about self into all aspects of a person's daily living.
R	An open source programming language used for statistical computation; most commonly used to develop statistical software.
Recommender systems	A system in which treatments, therapies and medications are recommended based on patient data.
Sentiment analysis	The use of algorithms to understand human feelings.
Structured data	Data that is organized in a predetermined structure.
Unstructured data	Data that does not prescribe to a predetermined structure, such as free text.

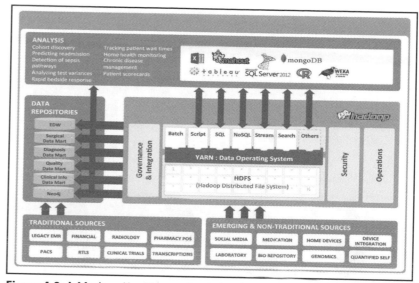

Figure 4-2: A Modern Healthcare Analytics Architecture.[7]

ones are not. Analytics is our new frontier and will be a requirement to manage large populations and hospitalized patients in real-time.

The core of a modern healthcare analytics architecture uses the same technologies that power Facebook, LinkedIn, Twitter, and Yahoo. These technologies are capable of ingesting large amounts of disparate data, storing that data, performing analytics, and serving up processed data for various use cases. This architecture does not replace the EHR, data repositories, or existing analysis tools; it is adjunctive and serves to supplement them. It can be considered the fourth stage of a healthcare analytics evolutionary process, as displayed in **Figure 4-3**.

Use cases for an analytics platform include monitoring social media for sentiment analysis to better understand the population's perception of our provider organizations. Marketing and communications can monitor and act accordingly. On the clinical side, an analytics platform is capable of monitoring our patients both in the hospital and at home in real-time, allowing for interventions much earlier. This platform will also support research and personalized medicine as it has the capacity for storing and analyzing genomic data. For a deeper dive on the technology, check out the suggested readings listed at the end of this chapter. (See common platform terminology in **Table 4-1**).

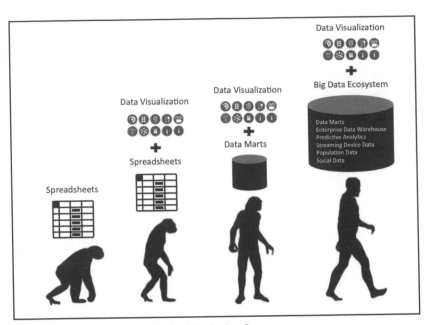

Figure 4-3: Healthcare Analytics' Evolution.[8]

Table 4-1: Modern Healthcare Analytics Platform Terminology.

Term	Description
Algorithm	A step-by-step of instructions for carrying out a process for problem-solving.
Anomaly detection	Data in a data set that does not match an expected or projected pattern.
Clustering analysis	Identifying data in a data set that is similar and grouping them together to understand the similarities as well as the differences within a data set.
Correlation analysis	An analysis of data to determine a positive or negative relationship.
Extract, transform & load (ETL)	A process in which data is extracted from a source, then transformed and loaded into a data warehouse.
Hadoop	An open source framework for the storage and processing of big data across a distributed file system.
HBase	Column-oriented data store allowing for fast access to data stored in HDFS (see HDFS).
Hadoop distributed file system (HDFS)	A file system for the storage of data across many computers.
Hive	A Hadoop data system that facilitates the interrogation of data stored in HDFS using Structured Query Language (SQL).

Data Visualization

Effective visualization of data from existing and emerging data platforms is often overlooked, leading to misrepresentation and misunderstanding. Looking forward, it is these very visualizations that will inform, alert, and educate clinicians and patients. Therefore, we need to understand the basic concepts to better prepare us to build not only our own data visualizations, but to assist in the development of clinician and patient-facing data visualizations. Data visualization technology is continually evolving. (Several sources are posted in the Suggested Reading section at the end of this chapter.)

Understanding how our sense of sight works is an essential first step in the data visualization process. Vision is our dominant sense and is tightly coupled with the process of thought. In his book, *Thinking, Fast and Slow*, Daniel Kahneman[9] presents two distinct processes of the brain:

- System 1 represents the automatic and intuitive thinking process.
- System 2 represents the thinking process that requires effort and attention.

You want to ensure that visualized healthcare data invokes automatic and intuitive thinking (System 1). You do not want viewers wasting time trying to figure out what information the data represents. (See **Figure 4-4** and **Figure 4-5**).

Figure 4-4 represents the presentation of data that requires a System 2 response. Tabular data and data poorly represented in a pie chart causes the viewer to rely heavily on thinking and very little on intuition, thus causing confusion and an out-of-balance state. Conversely, in **Figure 4-5**, the data is represented to evoke a System 1 response so that the viewer can, at a glance, understand the patient-waiting-time data.

When developing data visualizations, there are a few more points to consider. For example, consider a color palate that ensures your colorblind patients can read and understand it. Ensure your visualizations are reactive and can render regardless of the platform. We have all seen visualizations that worked well on a PC, but rendered poorly on tablets and smartphones.

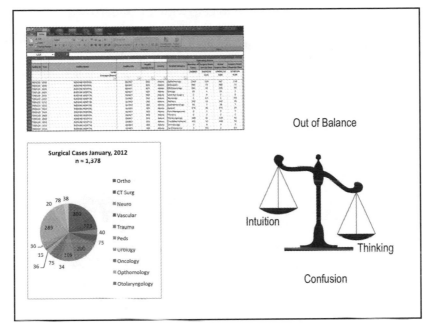

Figure 4-4: Out-of-Balance State.[8]

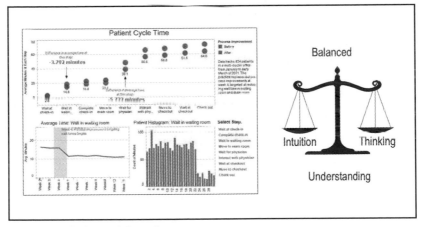

Figure 4-5: Balanced State.[8]

The infographic is emerging as a visualization modality that takes advantage of our System 1 response. Infographics convey an exceptional amount of data that is easily understandable at a glance. Florence Nightingale used infographics to visualize data. **Figure 4-6** is the infographic Nightingale created to help with the understanding of the causes of mortality during the Crimean War. The Rose Diagram is the precursor to what we now call a circular histogram.

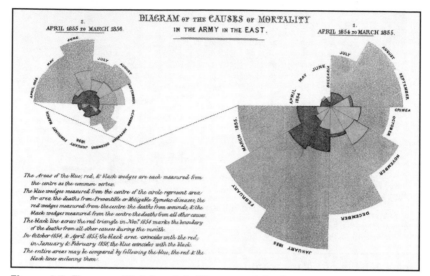

Figure 4-6: Florence Nightingale's 'Diagram of the Causes of Mortality in the Army in the East' (Public Domain).

POPULATION MANAGEMENT

Managing the care of populations entrusted to us is our looking-forward challenge. We are not only charged with developing technology solutions for the sick, but we now have to provide solutions to ensure optimal wellness for the entire population. This is no easy task and one that we must put time and effort into developing so that we do not repeat the mistakes of the past. Population management applications (PMAs) have to be multidisciplinary and include new team members such as navigators and care coaches. Care team members from hospitals, clinics, private practices, skilled nursing facilities, rehabilitation centers, home health, hospice, and community-based organizations, as well as patients, will be interacting with PMAs. They have to be interoperable, able to connect to various EHRs, patient portals, reference labs, and health information exchanges. This is but a small list of requirements to illustrate the need for nurse informaticists to be involved in the development lifecycle from the very beginning.

SUMMARY

To be successful with emerging technologies and their applications to healthcare, you must commit yourself to being a lifelong learner. Additionally, you must be vigilant and always on the lookout for new technologies, especially those outside of healthcare that can be adapted and applied to healthcare. In the past year I have moved away from following health IT bloggers and found that following technology-focused LinkedIn groups and tweets by health IT leaders keeps me current and provides direction on technologies to investigate.

With the continued dependency on analytics to evolve models of care, consider enrolling in a certificate or postgraduate program in healthcare analytics to keep up to date. Several organizations and universities offer online programs. **Table 4-2** lists a few programs to consider.

Table 4-2: Online Analytics Certificate and Graduate Programs.

Academic Organization	Program	Website
Georgetown University	Certificate	http://scs.georgetown.edu/programs_nc/CE0124/data-analytics?dID=5
University of California, Davis	Certificate	https://extension.ucdavis.edu/unit/health_sciences/certificate/healthcare_analytics/
University of California, Irvine	Certificate	http://unex.uci.edu/areas/it/predictive_analytics/
University of Maryland University College	Certificate	www.umuc.edu/academic-programs/certificates/predictive-analytics-graduate-certificate.cfm
Columbia University	Master of Science	www.cs.columbia.edu/education/ms/machineLearning
DePaul University	Master of Science	www.cdm.depaul.edu/academics/Pages/Current/Requirements-MS-In-Predictive-Analytics-Health-Care.aspx
North Carolina State University	Master of Science	http://analytics.ncsu.edu/
Northwestern University	Master of Science	http://sps.northwestern.edu/program-areas/Graduate/predictive-analytics/index.php

The next few years will bring tremendous change in the delivery of healthcare. As nurses and informaticists, we are uniquely positioned to lead this change through the careful and thoughtful application of technology. As healthcare technology leaders, we must be prepared and relevant, so stay informed and above all else, bring your own unique perspective to the design of future technology-enabled care delivery models. Attend technology conferences outside of healthcare, as there is much to be learned from other industries.

ADDITIONAL READINGS & RESOURCES

LinkedIn Groups

- Advanced Business Analytics, Data Mining and Predictive Modeling
- Big Data Visualization
- Big Data, Analytics and Data Science Training
- Digital Health
- Healthcare Analytics & Informatics
- Healthcare and Social Media
- Healthcare Technology Alliance
- Internet of Things
- Precision Medicine & Big Data in Life Science

Twitter Handles

- @amit_p
- @ANIAinformatics
- @Doug_Laney
- @dr_morton
- @drsanders
- @EdwardTuffte
- @fredtrotter
- @geek_nurse
- @KirkDBorne
- @N2InformaticsRN
- @Paul_Sonnier

- @skram
- @TechCrunch
- @travisigood
- @wareFLO
- @YvesMulkers

YouTube

- Demystifying Apache Hadoop in Five Pictures
  www.youtube.com/watch?v=xJHv5t8jcM8#t=706
- Hadoop 101: The Most Important Terms, Explained
  www.plottingsuccess.com/hadoop-101-important-terms-
  explained-0314/
- R Explained
  www.youtube.com/watch?v=M2u7kbcXI_k

Websites/Infographics

- Paul Sonnier
  www.pinterest.com/paulsonnier/digital-health-infographics-
  paul-sonnier
- Pinterest
  www.pinterest.com/search/pins/?q=healthcare%20
  infographics&rs=ac&len=10
- HIT Consulting
  hitconsultant.net/2014/01/31/best-healthcare-technology-
  infographics-of-2013
- HHS.gov
  www.flickr.com/photos/hhsgov/sets/72157633968047018

Suggested Reading

Barnett J. Forget What You Know: Jacob Barnett at TEDxTeen.
Posted Apr 9, 2012. www.youtube.com/watch?v=Uq-FOOQ1TpE.
Accessed Aug 15, 2014.

Börner K, Polley DE. *Visual Insights: A Practical Guide to Making
Sense of Data*. Cambridge, MA: MIT Press; 2014.

Few S. *Information Dashboard Design: Displaying Data for At-a-Glance Monitoring.* Burlingame, CA: Analytics Press; 2014

Hubbard DW. *How to Measure Anything: Finding the Value of "Intangibles" in Business.* Hoboken, NJ: John Wiley & Sons; 2014.

Kahneman D. *Thinking, Fast and Slow.* New York: Farrar, Straus and Giroux; 2011.

New York Department of Health. Delivery System Reform Incentive Program. Posted Apr 2014. www.health.ny.gov/health_care/medicaid/redesign/delivery_system_reform_incentive_payment_program.htm. Accessed Aug 15, 2014.

Wong D. 5 infographics to teach you how to easily create infographics in PowerPoint. Posted Feb 26, 2013. http://blog.hubspot.com/blog/tabid/6307/bid/34223/5-infographics-to-teach-you-how-to-easily-create-infographics-in-powerpoint-templates.aspx?source=hspd-promoted-tweet-5-infographics-blog-post-20140601. Accessed Aug 7, 2014.

References

1. Gladwell M. The Tipping Point: How Little Things Can Make a Big Difference. Boston: Little, Brown; 2000.
2. Davis K, Stremikis K, Squires D, et al. Mirror, mirror on the wall, 2014 update: how the U.S. health care system compares internationally. The Commonwealth Fund. Jun 16, 2014. Accessed Jul 21, 2014. Available at: www.commonwealthfund.org/publications/fund-reports/2014/jun/mirror mirror.
3. Gartner. Gartner's 2014 Hype Cycle for Emerging Technologies Maps the Journey to Digital Business. Posted Aug 11, 2014. Accessed Aug 11, 2014. Available at: www.gartner.com/newsroom/id/2819918.
4. Kemp, J. Gartner Research's Hype Cycle Diagram. Posted Dec 27, 2007. Available at: www.commons.wikimedia.org/wiki/File:Gartner_Hype_Cycle.svg.
5. CCS Insights. Wearable Forecast. Posted Aug. 1, 2014. Accessed Aug 32, 2014. Available at: www.ccsinsight.com/images/images/CCS_WW_wearables_forecast_August2014.pdf.
6. Lewin S. Holographic displays coming to smartphones. *IEEE Spectrum.* 2014; 51(8):13-15.
7. Sears J, Boicey C. Healthcare Does Hadoop. Posted Feb 2014. Accessed May 4, 2014. Available at: http://hortonworks.com/industry/healthcare.

8. Boicey C. Saritor: A big data ecosystem to advance research and clinical practice. Presented at Big Data in Health Conference, Apr 14, 2014: Boston.
9. Kahneman D. *Thinking, Fast and Slow*. New York: Farrar, Straus and Giroux.

CHAPTER 5

Nursing Informatics—
A Day in the Life

Edited by Tina Dieckhaus, MSN, RN-BC, NE-BC, CPHIMS, FHIMSS

As this book has made clear, nursing informatics (NI) as a speciality has evolved significantly over the decades. Nurses are making an exciting and profound impact in many areas of healthcare—from hospitals and academia to government and executive leadership.

This chapter—A Day in the Life—takes a look at the myriad professional roles taken by today's nurse informaticists, and is designed to provide for the next generation of nurses a better understanding of the potential and opportunities of this specialty. As Joyce Sensmeier states in the Foreword to this book, "…[A]ll nurses must be leaders in the design, implementation, and evaluation of the ongoing reforms to the health system. Nurses must understand that their leadership is as important to providing quality care as is their technical ability to deliver care in a safe and effective manner."

This chapter is divided into several broad categories—Education/Academia/Research; Clinical Settings; C-Suite; Consulting; and Government/Policy.

Though not a comprehensive list of all professions touched by NI, this chapter presents a look at the nurse informaticist as a leader.

EDUCATION/ACADEMIA/RESEARCH

Nursing Informatics Student—University of Colorado
Sarah Knapfel, BSN, RN, CCRN, MSN

- **Years in the Field:** 2 (Nursing informatics student)
- **Years in Current Role:** 6
- **Education:** Master's degree, Healthcare Informatics, University of Colorado Health Sciences Center; Bachelor of Science, Registered Nursing/Registered Nurse, Arizona State University College of Nursing; Associate's degree, Registered Nursing/Registered Nurse, Phoenix College.

My decision to pursue a degree in NI came about rather quickly. I never considered myself "technologically gifted," but realized the positive effects information technology (IT) had on the process of providing quality nursing care.

After having had the opportunity to work as a bedside nurse in many different arenas, I repeatedly found myself reflecting on my experiences and asking questions: What were we doing with all of the information being collected in the electronic health record (EHR)? How could we improve documentation methods for nurses? Could the implementation of this new product have gone better with improved planning?

Of course, my thoughts were not quite that sophisticated at the time, but my research led me down a valuable path into NI. I was fortunate enough to be accepted to an online program offering a Master of Science in Nursing degree with a healthcare informatics concentration. Not only was my journey as a full-time student beginning, but also my ambition to improve care delivery on a grander scale.

A Day in the Life…

A typical day as a nursing informatics student begins before my alarm clock has even gone off. *Ding!* I am immediately reminded that I neglected to silence my phone the night before, as a fellow classmate two time zones away checks in with the group before she ends her night shift at the hospital. She is reminding everyone to attend the video conference call scheduled for later that night to finalize our group project in our Decision Support and Data Management course. I appreciate the reminder and begin to work through my email from the comfort of my warm bed.

I have learned as a student in NI that due to the vast number of technologies evolving at such a rapid rate, subscriptions to health IT websites and memberships in professional organizations are essential for staying up to date on the latest news, policies, and research. This desire to stay informed consumes a lot of inbox space, but is found to be worthwhile when I discover an article related to new staffing measures for specialty areas, a subject that follows closely with my informatics practicum project. I forward the article along to my preceptor, and indicate that I would like to discuss this topic when we meet later that morning.

I am completing my internship, a total of 270 hours, with a clinical services group at the corporate headquarters of a large national health system. I arrive at my practicum site just before 8 a.m., and call into the first meeting of the day. I spend the next few hours taking notes and listening to issues discussed by representatives from various facilities in regards to increasing the adoption of an organization-wide workforce management system. When the conference call concludes, my passion for problem-solving is fueled, and I begin to research literature and frameworks that support how to successfully manage this change. I spend the rest of my morning collaborating with my preceptor to formulate a proposal that will ultimately improve the organization's education plan for charge nurses who use this system.

While taking time out for a quick lunch, I meet a friend who is a nurse and presently works in a clinical setting. She begins the conversation with a question I have been asked a dozen times before: "So, you're going to school for what exactly?"

I've practiced my answer to this question many times before, "It is a speciality of nursing that essentially bridges the gap between you, the bedside nurse using technology, and computer science experts in order to deliver safer, higher quality care." I feel a sense of accomplishment when she can easily understand my short, broad explanation. Of course, this approval is usually met with the comment, "It's great what you are doing—I'm just not that technologically gifted!"

After lunch, I spend the remainder of the day conducting an article analysis for an upcoming presentation at the American Medical Informatics Association (AMIA) Annual Symposium. This is not the first time I have volunteered my time as a member of a professional informatics organization. It's a great way to network with fellow students and AMIA members who have an understanding of my interests and specialty.

At the end of my day, I login to my online courses and continue to study our current module in preparation for tonight's meeting. Our group project, the use of a decision support tool relevant to a specific area of interest, has come together superbly. After thorough research, we are now justifying the use of an alert within the EHR to assist in properly preventing and treating hospital-acquired pressure ulcers based on facility policy and procedures. As complete as it is, we are well known for making last-minute updates to perfect our work. Being enrolled in an online program with nurses who work varying hours, and in varying time zones, has presented some scheduling challenges, as one can imagine. Over these past two years, we have become creative in our communication techniques—even if that includes an early morning group text message. After finalizing our project via videoconference and appointing a person to submit it, I say goodnight to my fellow classmates and breathe a sigh of relief. There are a few hours of relaxation before our next module begins in the morning.

Benefit and Value of a Nursing Informatics Degree

As my practicum comes to a close, I am beginning to understand the benefit and value this degree will have for me in the field. The specific scope and standards of practice in NI are the foundation for my graduate-level program. Over the course of the past two years, I have been introduced to curriculum material related to the application of e-health tools, nursing language and classification systems, system development and implementation, and database management.

Additionally, the courses I have taken in nursing research, theory, and policy will help strengthen my skill set as an advanced practice nurse. My decision to return to school and earn this type of specialty degree in nursing has exceeded my expectations. And finally, the supplementary skills I have attained, which include strategic organization, cohesive group communication, and effective time management, will further complement the healthcare informatics concepts I have been introduced to throughout the entirety of my program.

Informatics Nurse Specialist—Researcher
Susan McBride, PhD, RN-BC, CPHIMS

- **Years in Field:** 18
- **Years in Current Role:** 6
- **Education:** PhD, Nursing, Texas Woman's University; RN, BSN, Nursing, The University of Texas at Arlington.

As a traditional academic, a day in the life of a nursing researcher and faculty member offers a lot of variety for me. I have teaching responsibilities for online courses, including informatics, statistics, epidemiology, and policy courses at graduate school levels. My home residence is in Dallas-Fort Worth, and my home campus is in Lubbock, TX, over 300 miles from my home. I maintain a home office and fill a position as a full professor in a telecommuting role for which I travel across the state for teaching, research and policy work on behalf of Texas Tech University Health Sciences Center (TTUHSC). My office is a virtual one, for the most part.

In the teaching role, I have led the development of the statistics and informatics Doctor of Nursing Practice (DNP) courses, and participated in the team development of the epidemiology DNP course. I also led the development of the master's core informatics course, and we evaluated various projects for their effectiveness to reinforce competencies in both the DNP and masters essentials. We also used a mixed methods research approach to collect data qualitatively and quantitatively to inform the curriculum development for our master's curriculum; and we will be evaluating the effectiveness of the specialty courses for developing advanced skills in NI. As a clinical researcher with expertise in informatics, when I initially joined TTUHSC as an academic in 2009, the Office of the National Coordinator for Health Information Technology (ONC) released the ONC grants for the regional extension centers (REC) and health information exchanges (HIE). I designed and deployed the health IT strategy for the West Texas Regional Extension Center to support adoption, implementation, meaningful use, and evaluation of EHRs in 108 counties in west

Texas ($7 million funding). This grant was largely a program grant, but critical to the goal was to collect the right data to evaluate the success of our strategy in primarily a very rural west Texas setting. The initiative was to deploy EHRs in small practices, Federally Qualified Healthcare Clinics (FQHCs), and small hospitals (<100 beds). Our target was approximately 1,000 providers (including nurse practitioners), and 70 critical access and small rural hospitals across 108 counties of some of the most rural territory in the United States.

I served as founding director and had oversight for the development of the support services and evaluation methods of those services for the West Texas REC. In this role, I also served on various national Cooperatives of Practice (CoPs) in conjunction with the other 62 RECs across the country to establish and share best practices with respect to services provided. In addition, I have served in a consulting role to the CentrEast Regional Extension Center. Both the West Texas and CentrEast RECs are housed within the two Rural Institutes in Texas.

In community and advocacy contributions, I was appointed to and served on the Texas Medicaid Health Information Exchange state advisory committee for two years, and sat on the Nursing Workforces Studies Committee as a nursing researcher, as well as other various state advisory roles to the Department of State Health Services on the use of public domain data to inform public health and quality reporting.

We are currently working on research strategies within the TTUHSC Simulation Center to design methods for evaluating competencies on EHRs and to update clinical training scenarios with technology. We are examining safe medication practices and working with our University Medical Center to replicate medication errors within the simulated scenarios to reduce errors and promote best practices in computerized provider order entry (CPOE) and electronic bar-code administration.

In my role as Professor, I report to the Dean of the School of Nursing. With respect to the Regional Extension work I am involved with, I reported to the Senior Vice President at the Rural Institute. In summary, I find the role of an academic nursing informatics researcher to be rewarding work. The role provides opportunity to continue to improve practice through research, engage in the clinical practice setting with program activities, and foster the competency development of nurses and other healthcare professionals.

Adjunct Associate Professor
Beth L. Elias, PhD, MS

- **Years in Field:** 25
- **Years in Current Role:** 6
- **Education:** PhD, Instructional Technology, University of Virginia Curry School of Education; MS, Management of Information Technology, University of Virginia McIntire School of Commerce; BS, Computer Science, SUNY College of Technology.

With a background in computer science and health IT, I was not the most likely faculty candidate for a School of Nursing when I began this phase of my professional life more than five years ago. Formerly, my focus had been on computer systems administration, data management and health IT implementation. During that time, working on the frontlines of IT in healthcare, I began to see that nurses are the primary and largest group of health IT users. It seemed to me that if we wanted to make progress on integrating IT into healthcare, we needed to support, listen to, and work with professional nurses. It also became painfully clear to me that many of the health IT tools we were giving nurses were poorly designed, did not fit their workflow, and actually made nurses miserable more often than not.

Armed with this understanding and a commitment to come out from behind my computer monitor and into the real world, I started teaching nurses about health IT in the Master's of Science in Nursing (MSN) and Doctorate of Nursing Practice (DNP) programs. In this situation I expected to feel like a fish out of water, a techno-geek in a strange land of touchy-feely nurses. Quite a change, I thought, from the world of machines and lines of code that I had been living in until then.

The Masters-level students I taught were NI students, many of whom had been working in informatics roles and were returning to school to gain the next level of formal education ahead of board certification. Some students signed on because they felt that informatics was key to the future of nursing and they wanted to be a part

of that. The DNP students often saw health IT as a force to be reck-
oned with, but one that they were not fully prepared to integrate into
their practice.

With our MSN in Nursing Informatics students, several of my
stereotypes about the oil and water of nursing and techno-geeks fell
by the wayside. These nurses devoured every bit of health IT knowledge I could give them, clearly able to blend the caring aspects of their
nursing practice with the highly technical content of their course-
work. They were all about realizing the full potential of health IT to
advance nursing practice, improve patient outcomes and move their
organizations into the brave new world of IT-enabled healthcare. So
the two professional spheres seemed that they might not be mutually
exclusive after all!

It took working with the DNP students to fully drop the scales
from my eyes. Many of these students had not left paper charts behind
that long ago (or at all) when they returned to school. With some gen-
tle encouragement—that they could and would gain an understanding of health IT from the informatics course—they soon began to bite
off chunks of health IT content, swallow them whole and come back
for more. Wow, I thought, who knew that nurses would take to health
IT content like ducks to water? This kicked off a period of musing for
me on nursing, from an outsider's perspective and from the perspective of a professional who had felt our working worlds required very
different sorts of people.

Here are the three most important things that I came to realize:
1. Nurses are highly technical professionals who will instantly
   adopt anything and everything that can help them help their
   patients.
2. Nurses are the last safety check for patients and will not (and
   should not) tolerate increased risk to patients from badly designed technology—they will reject it.
3. Nurses are knowledge-based professionals who do not want
   a health IT application to be a substitute or a crutch for their
   critical-thinking skills.

I also realized some things about what nurses want from health
IT techno-geeks like me. They want good, usable, supportive and as-
sistive technology. They want our help using these tools effectively

and efficiently so they can do a better job taking care of their patients. They want us to show them some professional respect and see them as colleagues.

Nurses are highly skilled, knowledge-based, analytical and committed professionals. They are and will continue to be the largest single group of health IT users, and therefore the largest group of health IT customers (vendors, are you listening?). They are fully willing and able to understand IT if we, as techno-geeks, are willing to help them do so. So to nurses, adopt a techno-geek today. To techno-geeks, start thinking differently about nurses. To both, try actually talking to each other. Between us we can move mountains.

CLINICAL SETTINGS

Electronic Health Record Trainer—Hospital Setting

Lou Barr, MSN/MHA, RN

- **Years in the Field:** Three years, critical care tech in emergency department; seven years, emergency department nurse; one year, emergency department educator; two years, nursing informatics builder; one year, clinical informatics trainer
- **Years in Current Role:** 1
- **Education:** Bachelor of Science in Nursing; Masters of Science in Nursing, Master of Health Administration.

After graduating from high school in 1999, my nursing story began at Northwest Mississippi Community College, in Senatobia, where I completed my Bachelor of Science in Nursing (BSN) prerequisites. Upon completion, I transferred to Georgia Southwestern State University (GSW), where I obtained my first job in healthcare in the emergency department (ED) as a critical care tech/secretary. I graduated with my BSN degree in 2004, and began my nursing career at a small hospital in Georgia.

In 2005, I moved back to the Memphis area, where I was hired as an ED staff nurse for Methodist South Hospital, serving on the night-shift team. Less than two years later, I was promoted to the night shift supervisor, and at that time I went back to school to earn a Master of Science degree in Nursing and a Master of Healthcare Administration degree.

After I completed my graduate studies, I was given the opportunity to become the educator of the ED. My goal was to move up the management ladder, but I quickly realized that I did not want to be in nursing management at that point in my life, primarily due to employment politics. While in an ED meeting, an announcement was made that Methodist was looking for an informatics analyst to help with the ED's EHR. I applied for the job, was hired, and served Methodist for two years in this role. Because I enjoyed this job, I wanted to see what else was out there in informatics. After job searching for a few weeks, a friend told me about a Clinical Systems Trainer job at St. Jude Hospital. I thought this would be perfect for me because it's the best of both worlds. Fortunately, I was a good fit for the department and was hired.

Why is a Clinical Training Analyst Job the best of both worlds? I will answer this by first giving you a description of the position, telling you about the responsibilities and reporting structure, and finishing with a description of a typical day.

According to Payscale.com, the annual salary for a Clinical Training Analyst is between $41,526 and $85,918. Most clinical training jobs require that you have a Baccalaureate degree or higher and at least two to three years of experience in a training role. In addition to the education and experience, a clinical background is preferred but not required.

Training analysts train both clinical and non-clinical personnel how to chart and locate information in a hospital's EHR. In addition, they also train staff on new enhancements to the EHR. Training analysts use the classroom, web-based training, job aids, and on-the-job training to accomplish these tasks. Adobe Captivate, Adobe Photoshop, Microsoft PowerPoint, Microsoft Word, and Microsoft Publisher are a few of the programs that are used to create training materials. A good training program plays a key role for new employees' transitional phase into their new jobs. It also helps alleviate some fears that they may be facing when using a very expansive EHR.

A training analyst provides answers to questions the employees will face on the job, such as:

- How do I log into the system?
- Where is the information that I'm looking for?

- How do I place information into the record?
- If I mess something up, how do I fix it, or who do I contact?

Creating the job aids and training materials and performing the actual training of the many users is time consuming. One of the main advantages of having a team solely dedicated to training is that they have time to ensure quality training for employees and produce quality materials and job aids. Quality training helps users navigate through the EHR effectively and efficiently. Quality training materials help trainers be consistent and concise with their training. Quality job aids provide support in the times of need as users work in the EHR.

Even though having a team solely dedicated to training has its advantages, it also has its disadvantages. One of the main disadvantages is they are not in a clinical working environment. The training team is able to train employees on locating or charting information, but many times they do not know why they need to chart or locate the information. That is why a clinical background is preferred.

A good training team has members from different backgrounds. This is the reason that a clinical background is preferred and not required. As you read in my bio, my background includes working as an ED nurse. I'm very clinically oriented. I bring a clinical mind set to the training group. I'm able to answer the "why." However, I lack skills such as graphic design and adult training, which is why I depend on my team members who have more than 15 years' experience in these areas. As our teams goes through the day-to-day operations, we are able to use each other's strengths to develop and design high-quality adult education and training.

Now that you know more about what our clinical training analyst team does, let me lead you through a typical day. My day starts off around 8 a.m. I say "around" because one of the benefits of this job is flexibility. There is no real set schedule. The first thing I do each day when I get here is THANK GOD I made it through the crazy Memphis traffic. The second thing is check my calendar and email. As a training analyst, I go to many meetings and receive a lot of email. The email consist of training issues, people requesting job aids, and emails from users requesting or asking questions about training.

After replying to email, it is time for my first meeting: a design meeting about an upcoming enhancement to the EHR. Since training is key to successful implementation of changes to the EHR, training analysts are invited to many design meetings. After that meeting, I go to a process meeting about medication reconciliation. We play a key role in both design and process meetings since we are the ones in the EHR all the time and have face-to-face contact with the users. In these meetings we have an opportunity to provide input about training, process, and how the enhancements might impact the users.

Now it's time for lunch. Again, this job has a flexible schedule. I could go out, go to the cafeteria, or go home for lunch. Despite all these choices, I usually eat at my desk and work. On occasion, I will go out, but most of the time, I eat at my desk. Working in the ED, I really didn't get a lunch, so I usually ate on the run or out of a pocket, which means I'm used to working and eating at the same time. It's an old habit that's hard to break, and I'm a bit of a workaholic. My condition is getting better as I get older and smarter.

Throughout my lunch and after lunch, I work on job aids or tutorials. This is the thing I like about the job. I get to learn how to use new software programs such as Captivate, Photoshop, and Publisher. I didn't have a need to use any of these programs in the ED. After working a couple of hours on these, I might even browse the Internet, or take a stroll around campus. Coming from a busy environment and going to a desk job can be stressful. This is why it is important to take several mini-breaks throughout the day. (See, I told you my workaholism was getting better.) Later, it's time to teach a few clinicians how to chart and place orders. Another thing that is fun about training is that I interact with a multitude of medical disciplines, an avenue that enables me to learn about different fields in medicine. This is another example of why it's a good idea to have a clinical background: having something in common with the people you are training. It is finally time to go home!

I enjoy being a nurse whose title is now Clinical Training Analyst. The pay is good; a flexible schedule is great; and the greatest thing is being away from the bedside but still having interactions with the different medical disciplines. Is this job for everyone? No. Is this job for the nurse who wants to get away from the bedside, start his or her move up the corporate ladder, learn about informatics, but not lose contact with the medical disciplines? Yes. Who better to train users on how to use an EHR? A nurse. Why? Nurses are in the system more than anyone else, and they know how to interact with a multitude of different personalities. This is why a Clinical Training Analyst job is the best of both worlds.

Informatics Nurse Specialist—Hospital Setting
Minnie Raju, MS, RN

- **Years in the Field:** 9
- **Years in Current Role:** Four years as Clinical Documentation Lead, and two years as Liaison Lead (I am presently the Supervisor for both).
- **Education:** MS, Nursing Informatics, University of Maryland, Baltimore School of Nursing; BSN, University of Maryland, Baltimore School of Nursing; BS, Biology, State University of New York at Albany.

As the Nursing Liaison and Clinical Documentation (Clin Doc) Build Team Lead, I manage a staff that assumes a dual role. Under my direction, my team builds and integrates clinical and business functions into the hospital's information systems and services. By nurturing relationships within the nursing organization, we are able to effectively incorporate the goals of the IT department with that of the mission of the hospital.

As the Nursing Liaison, I am the primary intermediary between the IT department, clinical nurses, and research nurses. I provide clinical informatics support, communicating customer-oriented information that fosters clinical care and research. In my role as the Clin Doc Build Team developer, I facilitate the development of electronic clinical documentation to multidisciplinary clinicians and researchers throughout the hospital organization. This includes establishing process improvements/quality controls, implementing standardizations, and maintaining industry best practices of clinical standards of care. Clinical business and/or process improvement needs are identified and converted into functional requirements for implementation and integration into hospital information systems and services.

Both of my roles require an aptitude for effective collaboration and communication skills. This is done on a daily basis at organizational meetings, gathering requirements for creating and modifying clinical documentation, working with internal staff to ensure functional specifications are met, and reporting to the Deputy CIO of Clinical Informatics. These skills are also necessary when evaluating initiatives and projects for quality, benefit, efficiency, safety, and user satisfaction.

As an Informatics Nurse Specialist with a clinical background, my understanding of clinical process and workflow provides value to my hospital organization. I am able to serve as a conduit between clinicians and the IT department, which ensures that healthcare mandates are successfully incorporated into electronic clinical documents.

Informatics Nurse Specialist—Retail Health Setting
Susan Brown, MSN, FNP-BC, CPHIMS

- **Years in Field:** 20
- **Year in Current Role:** 4
- **Education:** BSN, Kent State University; MSN/FNP, Case Western Reserve University.

Imagine the amount of data generated by 20 million patient encounters over a 14-year period. Consider the implications of more than 2,500 nurse practitioners (NPs) practicing autonomously in more than 950 clinics, in greater than half the states in the country, as they complete 4 million visits each year. Clearly, there is no shortage of data; the challenge resides in translating that data into actionable information that informs and improves the practice of those NPs. What tools does a retail healthcare company leverage to accomplish such a translation?

My morning begins with a webinar, as our Clinical Decision Support team meets to review our EHR implementation strategy. We are in the process of transitioning from a proprietary electronic medical record to a patient-centric EHR from a leading vendor—a change that will elevate our ability to transform the vast amount of data entered daily from our providers into clinical and business intelligence to support our commitment to high-quality, affordable, accessible care.

Successful implementation of this new EHR requires a critical review of clinical documentation, understanding of principles of clinical decision support, and the translation of evidence-based clinical standards into structured data elements that can be queried through a reporting infrastructure.

As Director of Clinical Informatics, I assume the lead role as clinical subject-matter expert for the EHR implementation project, providing support and guidance to a team of NPs and application coordinators. Through the process of discovery, design, configuration, implementation, testing, and evaluation, we build a documentation platform that is customized to the unique practice of retail healthcare. A robust reporting infrastructure promotes on-demand clinical intelligence that—with appropriate expectations and feedback—allows providers to refine and improve their care delivery.

Those expectations and feedback mechanisms are part of our organization's quality improvement strategy, which is the topic of my afternoon webinar. An interdisciplinary team of clinicians from across the country—consisting of Master's- and doctorally-prepared nurses, NPs and physicians— convenes to discuss clinical quality measures in our retail healthcare setting. I've asked the team to consider measures for adoption in the coming year; the suggestions of the group members reflect the evolving nature of retail clinics, and underscore the pivotal role of NI in this practice setting, as we seek to integrate clinical quality measures that have historically been the purview of bedside nursing and primary care physicians.

As was the case with our EHR implementation project, my role includes translating data into actionable information. This time I lead the team through an exploration of the findings of my data evaluation and suggest recommendations for measurement metrics, based on my knowledge of analytics and informatics. I integrate the input from field and corporate leadership with the technical capabilities of our current and future EHRs to identify the best means of supporting our strategic quality goals. Our quality measures extend beyond the community base of our retail clinics to include promoting patient-centered medical care through affiliations with major medical systems across the country.

My last call of the day is with a nurse who is the program director for a university health system in a nearby state, with whom we have a clinical affiliation. Our public-private partnership aims to address gaps in care with chronic disease patients. As we review our project plan, we discuss integration of our patient records—something that will begin with the state's HIE and expand once our EHR implementation is complete.

As nurses, we are staunch advocates for data integration, without which our providers would not be able to address the patient's gaps in care or reinforce the patient's management plan. I share a draft timeline for our collaborative project, and suggest outcome measurements for each phase. Our next step is to present our recommendations to an interdisciplinary team of clinical and technology stakeholders for approval, after which I will continue to manage the project for our retail healthcare company.

In addition to project management, my position demands several core competencies, including expert knowledge of clinical care processes; use of enabling technology to standardize and optimize care delivery; proficiency in analyzing, developing, and re-engineering complex workflows and leveraging the capabilities of electronic systems to promote improved utilization and efficiency; and uniting interdisciplinary teams and individuals to support the clinical practice of our providers. Because I do not currently manage direct reports, my ability to connect teams is particularly important in my role: I must influence stakeholders and lead teams to execute and deliver, even without formal lines of authority.

As Director of Clinical Informatics, I report to our Chief Medical Officer through our Vice President of Medical Operations; I also work closely with our Chief Nurse Practitioner Officer, Vice President of Operations, Director of Quality, and Director of Information Systems. Collaboration within our organization's senior leadership is critical to understanding the needs and priorities of the company, and removes barriers to communication—allowing me to be more efficient in my short- and long-term projects.

As is the case with other clinical leadership roles within our organization, the position of Director of Clinical Informatics mandates both educational and certification requirements: a minimum of a

Master's degree in a healthcare discipline, national certification as a clinical provider (nurse practitioner, physician, or physician assistant), and national certification in information technology (CPHIMS is preferred).

The responsibilities of the clinical informaticist in a retail healthcare setting continue to develop and grow, as the lines between traditional primary care, hospital nursing, advanced nursing practice, community-based clinics, and regional medical systems dissolve. In an industry that strives to provide convenient quality healthcare while promoting coordinated care delivery, my role challenges me to integrate data and people to produce relevant clinical intelligence—a mantle I am honored to carry and hope to pass on to other nurses in the future.

Quality Specialist—Physician Office Setting
Rhelinda McFadden, RN, CPHIT, CPEHR

- **Years in Field:** 16
- **Years in Current Role:** 12
- **Education:** Associate Degree of Science in Nursing; BSN anticipated in 2016.

As a Quality Specialist Nurse with the Arkansas Foundation for Medical Care (AFMC), my role varies from practice to practice and healthcare provider to healthcare provider. AFMC is part of a team recently awarded by the Centers for Medicare & Medicaid Services (CMS) contract to be a Quality Innovation Network-Quality Improvement Organization (QIN-QIO), working under the regional umbrella of the TMF QIN-QIO (TMF Health Quality Institute, headquartered in Austin, Texas) for Texas, Arkansas, Missouri, Oklahoma and Puerto Rico.

AFMC's staff consists of more than 140 professionals in clinical medicine, data management, epidemiology, statistics and quality improvement. As a team leader for a multi-project focused team, I report directly to both a project manager and a departmental director.

Our mission is to improve the effectiveness, efficiency, economy, and quality of services provided to Medicare beneficiaries. By supporting healthcare professionals in Arkansas through education, outreach, sharing of best practices that have been successful in other areas, using data to measure improvement and through the active engagement of patients and families in their care, we improve healthcare for Arkansas.

Working in the rural primary care provider setting, the approach I take to my job is as different and unique as the office and healthcare provider with whom I am working. The majority of my time is spent functioning as a knowledgeable clinician, technology educator, and evaluator of data to define, maintain, and improve outcomes. I also mentor healthcare providers in becoming better technology consumers.

The majority of my work is defined by multiple state and federal initiatives. My priority is to identify methods to align and minimize the burden of participation in these initiatives on the rural practices I work with by being as informed as possible on the rapidly changing landscape of health IT.

Through the utilization of a consultative/face-to-face model of communication and education, I am able to implement quality improvement projects and activities for healthcare providers by developing an individualized plan for their practice and their specific EHR.

By providing expertise in the EHR systems most commonly used across our state, I serve as a knowledge resource and can facilitate the improvement of outcomes for targeted patient populations and/or specific clinical metrics. By being available to the healthcare providers in their practices, I can more effectively address their specific needs, which ultimately minimizes lost productivity and increases buy-in from providers and staff.

For me, it is important to understand the pulse of a practice and the healthcare providers within it. This allows me to have a better understanding of their unique approach to patient care delivery and the associated workflows. As the practice and I work together, we are able to define processes to measure the changes we are putting in place and ensure that they are sustainable. Because so many of these providers are still relatively new users of EHR technology, they are struggling with changes in the care delivery design and process automation which moves them away from the security of "the way we have always done it" and toward a more seamless healthcare delivery system design.

By engaging our healthcare providers and their staff in more meaningful utilization of their EHR technology to measure and monitor the data, we are able to improve clinical outcomes through clinical decision support and more effectively transform clinical practice.

My unbiased assessment of a practice offers an opportunity to address process changes, some as simple as utilizing staff to the maximum of their licensure to something a little more complex such as how to implement proactive strategies for planned care at every visit. Both of these strategies empower the healthcare team and improve the efficiency, quality, safety and effectiveness of the care being delivered.

In Arkansas, 75 percent of primary care providers are located in rural areas. These are primarily one- to two-provider practices with minimal clinical staff, resources, and time to research—or understand—current state and federal initiatives. Thus, identifying ways to align these initiatives to minimize the burden for providers is a priority.

As a quality specialist nurse and advocate for Arkansas healthcare providers and their practices, my job is to be a resource that is free to provide technical assistance, support, and information for all of these initiatives.

We are committed to be the resource of choice for our state and to serve as a first line of defense for healthcare in Arkansas.

Director of Informatics and Innovation/Manager— Healthcare Setting
Kimberly Ellis Krakowski, MSN, RN, CAHIMS

- **Years in Field:** 20
- **Years in Current Role:** 6
- **Education:** MS, Nursing, George Mason University; BS, Nursing, University of Mississippi Medical Center; CAHIMS, HIMSS.

As the Director of Informatics and Innovation at Inova Health System, I manage a team of 14 informatics analysts and senior informatics analysts and report to the Chief Nursing Information Officer and Chief Medical Information Officer.

We support the needs of five hospitals and more than 250 clinics with the mission to promote the quality, safety and usability of its clinical informatics systems and the medical informatics environment through strategic leadership and collaboration with all operational units.

It is my responsibility to prepare the clinical workforce for the use of technology so they may improve and deliver safe, effective clinical care. In addition, I oversee more than 30 departmental informatics transformation specialists (pharmacy, revenue, rehab, respiratory, case managements, and clinical outcomes).

I ensure strong, collaborative relationships and communication with the chief nursing officers, chief medical officers, chief financial officers, education department, information systems, training, human resources, stakeholders and vendors. I work to facilitate application integration and expansion of the system functionality throughout the health system. In our department, we value education and certification. And while it is not a requirement that employees of the informatics department are certified, it is strongly encouraged. Prep courses are provided and employees receive a bonus when certification is obtained.

Imagine visiting an amusement park. I start my day with a ride on the carousel, otherwise known as "rounding" in the office. It's a simple ride that many skip because it's not exciting, but it is genuinely part of my routine because it provides greater rewards than winning a giant panda after knocking down milk bottles. As I walk to the main attraction, I get easily distracted by phone calls and email just as kids are distracted by the cotton candy or music playing at all the rides. But ultimately I arrive at the amazing roller coaster, the Informatics Department (in this analogy). The Chief Medical Informatics Officer and Chief Nursing Informatics Officer support the organizational structure and provide the autonomy for me to lead the train that carries my team. When approaching the roller coaster, there is a sign that reads "*STAND TALL*," but it does not give a specific height. What it means is that to ride this train, or be a part of this team, you are required to stand tall for what you think is right at all times. There is also a sign that reads "CAUTION: The faint of heart should not attempt." It takes passion and commitment to be in this leadership role.

Having a Master's degree in Nursing Administration, certificates in Lean Process Improvement, certification as a builder in my EHR, and high emotional intelligence provides the knowledge and skills for me to lead my team.

My job in the lead car is to keep our goals in view and keep us on track, while knowing that sometimes things happen slowly, especially as we move forward to the top. I am also responsible for keeping the team aware of the twists and turns so that they do not get thrown for a loop. I know we can get turned upside down, but the momentum will keep us moving.

On a good day, everyone exits the ride smiling and laughing and wanting to ride it again. On other days, we may want to throw our arms in the air and scream! Often we find ourselves designing the next great roller coaster because we must be constantly ready to improve the way we do things!

As the Informatics Director, I strive to provide the strategic leadership in the development of workflows and ongoing continuous process improvement of clinical information systems, ensuring the successful application of informatics principles for its clinics, service lines and hospitals, while supporting organizational goals.

Sometimes, I trade my role in the lead car and instead walk around the amusement park in a clown suit passing out flowers, honking a horn, or giving high fives. Finding time to have fun and recognize others is just another role or hat the Director wears.

As the Informatics Director, I provide comprehensive leadership to complex projects. I use quality processes and evidenced-based practice to provide streamlined clinical solutions that meet the business needs related to clinical support applications, clinical work processes, and the redesign and enhancement of the core clinical IT platforms and workflows the core systems support.

It is critical to an organization's success to maintain up-to-date knowledge of trends and advances in the field of health IT, as well as new government and regulatory requirements for health information systems (HIS), including but not limited to Meaningful Use and core measures, then ensure their placement within the EHR. When it's time to leave the amusement park, I am still the Director of Informatics and Innovation. And I am a liaison and advocate to external health

systems, professional associations, and government/regulatory organizations as a subject-matter expert in HIS through presentations,
committee representation, and collaboration.

Vice President, Clinical Informatics—Long-Term Care Setting
Sylvia Rowe, MSN, RN-BC, LNHA

- **Years in the Field:** Worked with Ethica Health and Retirement
  Communities for 25 years in long-term care, beginning as a
  Certified Nurse Assistant; have been a Registered Nurse for 21
  years; and served in various roles in the long-term care setting
  including Director of Nursing, Case Management, Care Plan
  Coordinator, and many other roles.
- **Years in Current Role:** 3
- **Education:** MSN, Informatics, Walden University; BSN, Nurs-
  ing, Georgia College and State University.

To understand the role of the nurse informaticist in long-term care
(LTC), one must first understand that long-term care spans a variety
of settings including assisted-living facilities, personal care homes,
home health, hospice, skilled-nursing facilities, and LTC post-acute-
care hospitals. Roles and responsibilities will differ in each of these
settings due to variations in structure within the wide array of settings
classified under the umbrella of LTC.

The following description will focus primarily on the role of the
nurse informaticist working in the skilled-nursing facility (SNF) setting. It would be rare in the LTC setting to find the nurse informaticist
working in a local setting. More commonly, you will find the nurse informaticist working in a regional or corporate support role. The nurse
informaticist's reporting structure will differ from organization to organization as well. Commonly, the nurse informaticist may report to
the IT department, clinical practice, or compliance office. The nurse
informaticist may be isolated in the department or may have direct
reports such as health information management specialists, nursing
analysts, implementation specialists or support associates.

A day may find the nurse informaticist in the SNF setting conducting a facility walkthrough to inventory hardware and software or
assess wireless coverage to identify any gaps in these areas for current

or future needs. This walkthrough will facilitate a need for the nurse informaticist to ensure IT has a clear understanding of operational and clinical needs for the SNF and that operations and clinical areas have a clear understanding of any costs associated with filling in the gaps and the impact of gaps on workflow.

In addition to assessing needs and gaps, the nurse informaticist has a responsibility to collaborate with operations personnel, ensuring that replacement and maintenance of hardware and software are considered in the annual budget review process.

On another day you may find the nurse informaticist in the SNF setting, bringing user group(s) together to evaluate current software to determine if the software is meeting the current end-user needs, or if it is being utilized to its full potential. This may lead to working with end users and the vendor to develop additional training or sunsetting an application.

The nurse informaticist working with a user group(s) will also be responsible for guiding and directing product selection if a change in software is deemed necessary or if needs are identified outside the scope of what the current software is capable of providing. This may result in the nurse informaticist leading an implementation team for new software. Additionally, with growing interest around telemedicine brought about by need for access, cost control and quality, the nurse informaticist in LTC will share responsibility for implementation, oversight and management of telemedicine programs.

Any given day will be filled with multiple calls and meetings, both internal and external. Calls for the nurse informaticist may include general questions from end users, contract discussions with vendors, project management calls, collaborating with other providers such as a doctor's office, hospital, or home health agency to help support provider initiatives.

The day includes various meetings for the nurse informaticist as well, such as security and privacy, compliance, project planning, organizational strategy, vendors, quality assurance and performance improvement, and end-user education and support. The day may also include the task of gathering and analyzing data, developing educational programs on new technology or processes, and general collaboration with IT to ensure everyone is working toward the same goal.

The nurse informaticist in LTC can bring value to many areas in this setting when skills and training are utilized effectively. As a clinician, the nurse informaticist can help prepare the organization for value-based purchasing, participation in accountable care organizations (ACOs), and providing the data needed to effectively collaborate with other healthcare providers moving forward. The nurse informaticist in LTC can be a leader within the organization by assessing current workflows to identify ways technology can be effectively and efficiently employed to enable safe, cost effective, quality patient care through identification and elimination of redundancies in workflow processes.

Educational and clinical background requirements may vary from organization to organization. In many instances, this role will be filled with someone possessing a Bachelors degree in nursing and experience in LTC. Other organizations may require more specific training and education in IT, business management, and/or NI. Someone in this role should, at a minimum, possess a nursing degree and have a working knowledge of basic IT principles.

C-SUITE

Chief Nursing Informatics Officer—Inpatient/Ambulatory Care Setting
Mark Sugrue, RN-BC, FHIMSS, CPHIMS

- **Years in Field:** 25 years
- **Years in Current Role:** One year
- **Education:** BS, Biology, Psychology, University of Massachusetts Boston; BSN, Nursing, Regis College; MSN candidate (May 2015).

As the Chief Nursing Informatics Officer (CNIO), my role spans both the inpatient and ambulatory environments. I am responsible for strategic and operational nursing leadership in the selection, development, deployment, re-engineering, and integration of IT to support clinicians and patient service. In this role I report directly to the Chief Nursing Officer (CNO), and am a member of the hospital administrative leadership and nursing executive teams.

As the CNIO, I believe that it is important that my role span all practice areas and not be isolated to the inpatient or ambulatory environments. Decisions I make impact nursing practice and therefore must be first and foremost grounded in the institution's nursing practice model and philosophy. While some variation in nursing practice may exist between the inpatient and ambulatory environments, it is important to continually return to the core nursing professional practice model, which is the same across all environments of care.

The reporting structure of the CNIO is evolving and varies greatly from institution to institution. In a research study conducted by Sarah Collins, RN, PhD, nurse informatician at Partners HealthCare Systems and instructor in medicine at Harvard Medical School/Brigham and Women's Hospital, it was found that the partnerships across the nursing structure, medical structure, and Information Services (IS) structures are integral.[1] To achieve successful outcomes, the research suggests that informatics needs to be seen as a clinical project in collaboration with IS.

According to Collins and her team, "This requires leaders who understand the clinical needs and also can see the patient safety implications, while having an appreciation for the technical complexity of the work."

In my role, for example, I have a direct reporting relationship to our CNO. Since assuming the role, I have worked hard to establish a collaborative working relationship with our IS leadership. It is my opinion that this governance structure clearly puts the emphasis for my practice and leadership on nursing and patient care, while allowing for a strong connection to our IS team.

In many ways, my day-to-day work is guided less by our governance structure and more by the framework of the American Nurses Credentialing Center's Magnet Recognition Program®. The Magnet framework includes transformational leadership; structural empowerment; exemplary professional practice; new knowledge; innovation and improvement; and empirical outcomes. The Magnet elements of innovation and improvement and empirical outcomes, for example, are fundamental to our efforts related to the implementation of our new EHR.

This implementation has provided many opportunities for the voice of nursing to be heard and to influence system design, build and implementation. Ambulatory nursing practice, for example, will greatly transform as we migrate from our paper-based processes to a technology-rich care delivery environment across all ambulatory practice settings. On a daily basis I am working with our teams to develop innovative and transformational approaches to care delivery that are enabled by our new technology solution. Likewise, we are continually evaluating the empirical outcomes that we can achieve. Reduction in errors, improved safety, and improved patient and staff engagement are just a few of the key performance indicators that guide our daily work and help us measure performance.

Whether working on issues related to our current environment or leading our migration toward a new EHR, I believe that the most important role I play is a leadership role. Transformational leaders combine strong academic preparation along with years of management experience and skills to develop the leadership capacity of team members by providing both support and challenges. CNIOs are typically prepared at the Masters or Doctoral level and, like myself, bring 20 or more years of applied nursing and informatics experience to the table. Transformational leaders inspire team members to embrace a shared vision and encourage the use of innovative problem-solving methods.

In conclusion, the role of the CNIO is evolving and rapidly becoming recognized as a mission-critical member of the healthcare leadership team. The CNIO role adds value by elevating the voice of nursing and informatics to the C-suite and ensuring that clinical workflows are understood and patient care delivery is optimized.

REFERENCE

1. Cadet JV. Governance for nursing informatics: who dictates what? Clinical Innovation + Technology. Mar 27, 2013. Available at: www.clinical-innovation. com/topics/analytics-quality/governance-nursing-informatics-who-dictates-what?nopaging=1.

Chief Nursing Information Officer—Healthcare System
Patricia Mook, MSN, RN, NEA-BC

- **Years in Field:** 34
- **Years in Current Role:** 14 months
- **Education:** BSN, Nursing, University of Vermont; MSN, Nursing Administration, George Mason University; Post Graduate Certificate, Leadership, Villanova; Advanced certified, Nursing Executive Advanced; BC, American Nurses Credentialing Center; Doctoral in Business Administration, California Southern University (enrolled).

I have the privilege of being the first CNIO for Inova healthcare system. It is my job to provide visionary leadership and establish direction for a comprehensive clinical informatics and education program with a primary focus on clinical and nursing practice, administration, research and academic partnership in support of interdisciplinary patient-driven care.

In an effort to ensure we are a high-reliability organization for patient care, I strive to provide leadership within operational informatics and educational programming to support organizational goals. I oversee and lead all aspects of staffing, including workforce planning, recruiting, performance management, career development and compliance for the informatics and Inova Learning Network.

The Director of Informatics and Innovation, who manages 68 full-time equivalents (FTEs) who are Informatics Analysts and Senior Analysts, is one of three direct reporting leaders. The Director of the Inova Learning Network and Simulation department, which includes ten FTEs in addition to the Manager of Epic Training with 45 FTEs, also reports up through the CNIO. I matrix report up to the Senior Vice President and CNO and the Chief Medical Information Officer (CMIO) for the Inova Health System.

This reporting structure allows for excellent communication to the nursing operations side, the medical informatics contingency, and the IT areas. The CMIO reports directly to the Chief Technology Officer (CTO) for the health system. Together we provide for an interdisciplinary team that leads strategy, development and implementation of IT to support nursing, nursing practice, clinical applications and clinical/operational decision making, in addition to incorporating the operational needs that encompass and support revenue-cycle informatics for five Inova hospitals and six Alliance hospitals, in addition to more than 250 clinics. My leadership team's primary focus is to maximize the ability of nurses and their interdisciplinary colleagues to use informatics and technology in a safe, efficient and effective way that is evidence-based and grounded in education and research.

As the CNIO at Inova Health System, it is important that I focus on continual learning and education at all levels. I have a Master's Degree in Nursing Administration, am Nurse Executive Advance-Board Certified, and am a build-certified analyst for our EHR. Inova requires that all chief nurse executives have a minimum of an MSN degree and an advanced nurse executive certification. It is preferred that the person holding this position has a doctoral degree, and I am presently enrolled in a Doctoral in Business Administration program. My certification as an analyst gives me the ability to truly understand what is capable for the end user as we make decisions regarding the clinical documentation build.

At Inova, IT is seen as an integral part of care delivery and my vision is to build the knowledge skills and experience of not only my nurse informaticist but each and every nurse in the use of our IT systems. This requires a unique set of competencies that we incorporate into our professional development of nurses and all end users of our EHR.

As the CNIO, I champion the professional development of clinicians to ensure that their core competencies include computer skills, informatics knowledge and skills, and risk identification knowledge. Pre-employment training is essential, but in order to keep up with the unending pace of changes, we had to think quickly and initiate a unit-based expert to assist in the development of knowledge and skill in the safe use of the EHR.

Here at Inova, I addressed this with the development of a collaborative "Super User" program that supports end users locally in their hospitals and clinics. They champion the adoption of new workflows and technology and serve as coaches to their clinical colleagues. I serve as a cheerleader to the ongoing education and certification of many of these Super Users by advocating for 50 nursing analysts to attend local training to support certification in an effort to improve competencies.

I see my role as CNIO as one that creates a climate that promotes staff engagement, and I hope to inspire nurses to adopt innovation as they think about their work at the side of a patient. All this is being considered in order to impact the overall outcomes of those whom we are privileged to serve every time and with every touch of our patients.

With the most recent operational informatics infrastructure that has been developed, we strive to be intermediaries between the clinicians and the technical build teams. Under my strategic direction, the informatics department coordinates interdisciplinary clinical input with design, testing, implementation, and evaluation of our applications. We support the development of clinical protocols to ensure that required changes are made to clinical documentation and order sets. Another area of engagement is focused on what is needed to meet Meaningful Use requirements as they change at an astronomical speed.

I work collaboratively with the CMIO and the VP of Enterprise Applications to design and redesign the EHR as we follow our guiding principles. Our goal is to provide standardization and get to a OneInova process. My job is to persistently advocate for nursing practice and clinical documentation to be on an agreed-upon standard and to insist upon following best practice as it is defined by the organization. The design of nursing clinical documentation falls under the direction of the CNIO and the provider design team falls under the direction of the CMIO, with informatics team members ensuring that the OneInova goal is kept in sight at all times.

I also provide strategic direction to the Inova Learning Network (ILN) and the Epic training team. Our vision as an organization is to use more simulation and assist with outreach training. By strategizing with the System CNO, the Director of the Medical Residency Program, and the Director of the ILN and Simulation, we are driving the development of a state-of-the-art Simulation Center where we will use innovative ways to accomplish scenario-based interdisciplinary teaching/learning.

I see my work culminating in the advocacy for superior patient outcomes, which often depend on the engagement of clinical end users in the design of our applications, while providing an atmosphere for research that will foster evidence-based care and best practices. This is supported through the IT Research Council, which has developed under my direction.

I see my position as a valuable asset to the organization at a time when change is moving at warp speed. I was recruited into this position because of my clinical and operational background. The goal was to lead the change from a very fragmented multiplatform EHR, to one integrated system for five hospitals and close to 200 ambulatory sites. This endeavor needed to transition in less than two years. We were able to successfully build out the clinical documentation for all required areas. I lead the validation sessions, design teams, and all clinical build through testing and the implementation of the product.

The measurement of success has been determined by our successful completion of Stage 1 Meaningful Use, the improvement of Core Measure indicators, a decrease in mortality, and improvements in multiple true north goals for the organization. As exemplified with this EHR implementation, as the CNIO, my value is measured by how I drive innovation, through interdisciplinary collaboration, and support of end-user professional development in the areas of informatics, with the ultimate goal of optimal outcomes always in sight.

CONSULTING

Nursing Informatics Consultant—Software Company
Patricia Foley Daly, DNP, RN-BC

- **Years in the Field:** 25
- **Years in Current Role:** 4
- **Education:** DNP, University of Kansas.

A consultant is defined by *Merriam-Webster Dictionary* as "one who gives professional advice or service." Typically, the NI consultant is someone outside the organization who is hired, as an expert, to address a specific need. The consultant is usually employed by a larger organization such as a software supplier or consulting organization. In the field of nursing informatics, consultants possess expertise in a wide variety of areas—EHR selection, clinical transformation, solu-tion implementation, quality improvement, benefits realization, and workflow redesign among them. A consultant will address any issues or needs for which the organization has hired them.

For a consultant in a software supplier organization, the NI roles are varied as well. For the purposes of this book, the consultant role discussed here will be the one responsible for implementation of the EHR. This role is often described as a clinical strategist. The clini-cal strategist is engaged in the implementation of all clinical software solutions. Many other roles are engaged in the project as well. The clinical strategist is responsible for working with nurse executives and other key nursing personnel to ensure a successful project.

The first activity the clinical strategist is involved in during an implementation is to understand the clinical objectives to be realized in the future state. This is important in the definition of the benefits to be realized post-implementation. As part of this process, the cur-rent-state baseline will be documented. The clinical strategist assists the organization in these activities.

The next activity is the current-state review in which the current clinical processes are reviewed for comparison to future state. This involves discussions with all clinical areas to understand their current processes. Data are collected via interviews, observations, and collec-tion of current materials used for documentation. Clinicians are ob-served delivering care to validate the data obtained during the inter-views. The clinical strategist leads these data-gathering activities. He or she is responsible for ensuring all processes are documented and all clinical areas represented. Often he or she serves as a "translator" for the non-clinical members of the implementation team.

The next step in the implementation process is the design and build of the system. This is based on the future state and scope of the project. The scope is typically defined during the early planning phas-es of the implementation. During the design and build phase of the project, the clinical strategist works with the nursing team to ensure they understand the design and validate the build. The clinical strate-gist makes changes to the system build as necessary based on client feedback. This is an iterative process. Once the build is complete, test-ing begins. The clinical strategist assists the client in the development of test scripts. There are usually various levels of testing—unit and integration testing. During the testing phase, the clinical strategist assists the client as their staff work through the test scripts.

Throughout all these phases, the clinical strategist provides feedback and guidance to the nursing executive team on the progress of the project. The final activity prior to conversion to the new system is training. Although this is typically the client's responsibility, many activities must occur prior to training to ensure its success. The clinical strategist is responsible for training the subject matter experts who will then perform the training for end users. He or she is also responsible for assisting the nursing project team in the training planning.

Training is a significant event that is logistically challenging and must be planned for many months in advance. Conversion requires the support of the entire team. The clinical strategist plays a significant support role for the client team in their support of the nurses and other clinicians. The clinical strategist also assists in staffing the central area where the project team resides, fielding issues and dispatching resources as needed throughout the organization.

After conversion, the clinical strategist performs the post-conversion assessment. This again involves interviews and observations of the clinical processes that were automated. The benefits expected are measured or compared to the pre-implementation levels. This data is shared with the nursing leadership.

The clinical strategist is a key member of the team and integral to the activities described above. He or she understands the current state and clinical processes of the organization. In addition, he or she understands the new system/software being installed. So he or she plays a key role in assisting the staff to understand the new workflows and integrating the software into the organization to meet their goals.

Furthermore, the clinical strategist serves as a liaison to the nursing executive team throughout the project. This role is pivotal to the success of the implementation. This is just one example of the important roles nurse informaticists play in the consulting realm.

The clinical strategist is a member of the larger implementation client team. He or she is also a member of the clinical strategist consulting team at their software organization. The reporting structure of this team is very similar to the clinical reporting structure in a hospital. These individuals are predominantly nurses who report up to a nurse manager and, ultimately, a nurse executive. The strategist is the individual who works directly with clinicians at the client sites. So the role is comparable to the bedside nurse in the hospital. From an education perspective, they are Bachelor-prepared nurses at a minimum. Some have advanced degrees in informatics as well. Certification is preferred but not typically a requirement. The software supplier I work for sponsors certification courses that are open to all nurses in the organization. Advanced degrees and certification denote an individual's desire to advance his or her learning and expertise in the informatics realm.

Nursing Informatics Consultant—Consulting Company
Lisa Anne Bove, DNP, RN-BC

- **Years in the Field:** 20
- **Years in Current Role:** 15
- **Education:** DNP, Nursing Informatics, Duke University; Post-Master's, Nursing Admin, Villanova University; MSN, Critical Care Nurse Specialist; BSN, Registered Nursing/Registered Nurse, Widener University.

I start my work week with an early Monday morning plane ride to my client. In my carry on bag, I have everything I need for the week—sneakers, work clothes, toiletries and something comfortable to wear after work hours. In my briefcase, I have everything I need in an office—computer, smartphone, power cords, paper clips, sticky notes, pens, hand sanitizer and head phones. In my head, I have experience implementing clinical systems, workflow redesign and system optimization. I will return home again on Thursday night or Friday. I am a healthcare informatics consultant.

While travel can be tedious at times, my weekly commute is often shorter than many of my peers. In addition, I frequently get to work from home on Fridays and during major holiday weeks like Thanksgiving or Fourth of July. Many ask why anyone would do this, and the answer is the work. As an informaticist, I help my clients implement EHRs and redesign work process impacted by technology.

As a consultant, I bring outside experience and a neutral view to complicated changes in an organization. I partner with experts within the organization and help them get their voices heard. I often deliver the difficult messages without the same risks as an employee who has to continue to work within the organization whether the project succeeds or not. My day-to-day work varies with each project. I have implemented clinical systems, developed return-on-investment and cost-of-ownership scenarios, led teams to design best-practice future state of systems to meet regulatory requirements, as well as developed training plans for entire hospital systems rollout, strategic plans of IT departments, and hospital acquisitions. Each project can be like a new job!

Consultants can bring value in several ways. The first is that consultants are experienced with leading multiple projects. They may have done the same project at multiple client sites or with multiple vendor solutions and have seen a variety of ways to do the project. In this way, they can share the experiences and help the client choose the solution most likely to succeed in their environment. The second is that consultants go where the work is and are temporary.

For example, when an organization implements a new EHR, they need numerous team members—more than they will need to support the software after it is in use. Consultants can supplement staff and usually do not require additional education on the vendor's software, but can instead 'hit the ground running.'

My reporting structure changes from project to project. Within the company, I report to a director who leads the group methodology and helps consultants find positions to fit their skills. On the project, consultants can report at almost any level. Often consultants follow the same reporting structure that other employees do. Analysts often report to managers in finance, IT, and/ or a clinical department. Project managers tend to report to managers in IT. Advisory consultants tend to report to C-level executives.

The educational requirements for a consultant are similar to those for hospital employees, although more is better when it comes to certifications and education. For clinicians who are functioning in consulting roles, a Master's degree is helpful, but not required, as most clients see education as a credential demonstrating experience and skill.

Certification in a specialty like nursing informatics by the American Nurses Credentialing Center (ANCC) and/or a vendor product is also helpful to increase the possible opportunities. In addition, I am frequently asked if I have Project Management Professional (PMP) certification, as this is a standard in the industry for project and program managers, a role I frequently fill. While none of these certifications or advanced degrees guarantees a higher salary in consulting, they can help.

The key skills that consultants need are similar to those needed by nurses—change management, facilitation, communication, documentation and experience working in complex healthcare organizations. When I first start a project, I work to learn about the organization's culture and how decisions are made. I get to know all the stakeholders—the people on or interested in the project. During this phase, I also work to learn the goals of the project, what the organization expects to gain from the project, and what, if anything, could happen if the project fails.

My next step is to plan how the team and I will accomplish the work. Sometimes the planning is the primary work and sometimes I get to actually help carry out the plan. One of the things that I try to bring to each project is lessons learned from previous projects, articles and/or experts in the field. It's hard to see the same issues played out over and over again with various clients. While every organization is different, communication and clear, concise decision making are issues at many client organizations. Showing examples of how to present data in ways to support decision making or communication, such as dashboards, communication matrixes or executive status reports, can help. Facilitating meetings with experts from other organizations so they can share best practices or brainstorm possible solutions is also helpful. Informatics can help improve patient care by presenting patient information to all caregivers, aggregating findings across patients and reducing redundancies in care.

Because I am a consultant, as the project draws to a close, so does my time at the client site. Sometimes, I am ready to leave if I feel my work is done. Sometimes, moving on is hard, especially if there is a lot of work still to be done. Hopefully, before I leave, I have transitioned the skills and tasks needed to continue to move data along the continuum to knowledge and eventually wisdom. As I pack my bags to head to another client, I add the new information and lessons learned to my bag of tools.

GOVERNMENT & POLICY

Policy Analyst
Darryl W. Roberts, PhD, MS, RN

- **Years in the Field:** 25
- **Years in Current Role:** 2
- **Education:** PhD, Public Policy, University of Maryland Baltimore County; MS, Nursing Informatics/Public Policy, University of Maryland Baltimore; Graduate Certificate, Public Policy, University of Maryland Baltimore County; BSN, Nursing, University of Maryland School of Nursing; ASN, Nursing, Essex Community College; LPN, Practical Nursing, Johnston School for Practical Nursing.

Health IT is an incredible field. It offers the perfect combination of tension between what clinicians want to see happen and what technology is capable of making happen. Tension breeds dissatisfaction; dissatisfaction breeds innovation; and innovation temporarily satisfies. It's wonderful. Think about it—nurses, physicians, pharmacists, and so many others seek efficiency, better processes, and easier and less socially invasive ways to get work done. Everyone wants better patient outcomes, reasonable reimbursements for good work, and strong incentives for excellent work. Underneath it all, many want the coolest gadget, too. Health IT vendors are willing to provide solutions to satisfy everyone. All purchasers need to do is find a way to pay the prices, which can range from very reasonable to incredibly expensive.

Attenuating and facilitating all of these interactions at a micro level are the individual actors: clinicians, vendors, payers, and—increasingly—patients. At the macro level, wonks come out to play. I am a wonk.

"What is a wonk?" you ask. Wonks are the people who have an in-depth knowledge of the interactions around a certain aspect of public policy. They know the people in that arena. They attend the meetings, review the papers, write reviews, and respond to opportunities for public comments on federal rules and regulations, among myriad other things. My particular areas of wonkiness are healthcare quality and health IT. Some of us are physicians, economists, and political scientists. I am a registered nurse (RN). You don't necessarily need a higher education to be a wonk, but it does help. A considerable number of people in this area of expertise have graduate degrees and professional degrees; many are doctorally prepared.

What I learned over the past 25 years is that healthcare, healthcare research, and health IT are not about physicians, nurses, or even the all-knowing government. They are really about the patient. Yes, it sounds trite. I apologize for that, but it is actually, finally true.

Organizations like the Agency for Healthcare Research and Quality (AHRQ) and the Patient Centered Outcomes Research Institute (PCORI) have forced those of us who depend on contract funding for our livelihoods to include the patient's voice in our planning, implementation, and evaluation designs. It makes perfect sense, but it is a reach for many in my generation of clinicians and researchers. We were trained to ask patients questions and attempt to meet their needs, but we were never trained to give them control. Today, many are taking charge of their own care. Technology has made that happen.

I got the basis of my health IT, quality, and public policy knowledge from school, but I learned so much more by doing the work and working with others in the field. Meeting experts—whether they are subject-matter experts in a certain field or patients and patient advocates—and socializing with them is a huge part of learning and working in these fields.

Jobs like informatics, policy analysis, and policy advocacy require presence. I learn so much from conferences, like the Annual HIMSS Conference & Exhibition and the American Medical Informatics Association's Annual Symposium, and from meetings, like the ONC's Health IT Policy Committee (HITPC) and the Bipartisan Policy Center's Learning Health System Committees. Attendees and presenters at these meetings are there to share and learn how to make the systems around us better for patients and clinicians alike.

Over the past few years, a considerable part of my work has been in public policy as it relates to health IT and healthcare quality. Many reading this might not think of this as NI. Nursing informatics is the confluence of cognitive science, information science, and computer science applied through the lens of nursing science. It focuses on how nurses use, implement, manage, and maintain information systems within a healthcare setting.* Public policy sets the boundaries and standards for health IT and informatics. When I worked for the American Nurses Association (ANA), I kept track of changes in policy that might affect nurses and patient care. In my new role, I write the quality measures that the government uses to assess the quality of care and I conduct research around the effectiveness of that care. This is nursing informatics.

A Day in the Life

My charge in writing this essay is to discuss a day in the life of a policy analyst and advocate for the ANA. In this role, I review, respond to, and inform public policy that resides in the confluence of health IT and healthcare quality. Additionally, I advise ANA's leadership on methods of maximizing existing policy and recommend future policy improvement. In addition to my full-time work, I am an adjunct professor at the University of Baltimore's Health Services Management Program, where I teach undergraduate and graduate non-clinicians the essential roles and tools for managing healthcare systems. I also teach adjunct at the Stevenson University Graduate and Professional School, where I teach quality management to nurses. These roles require me to remain at the cutting edge of knowledge.

Today Is a Tuesday in January

The day starts simple and ordinary. My iPhone awakens me at 5:30 a.m. and gives me immediate access to the *Commonwealth Fund e-Alert*, *Modern Healthcare A.M.*, and *Becker's Hospital CIO Report* feeds. At a glance, they tell me about the latest events in the world of health IT. Paging through them alerts me to a new *Commonwealth*

---

* Turley James P. Toward a model for nursing informatics. *IMAGE: The Journal of Nursing Scholarship*; 28, no. 4 (1996): 309-313.

blog post on Insurance Marketplaces that Promote Quality Improvement (http://bit.ly/1lqvGNd), which concludes that we have a long way to go. *Modern Healthcare* tells me that there is hope for relief from the two-midnights rule for hospitals (http://bit.ly/1ojSMj9), but concludes that hospitals could benefit from coaching on how to code better to maximize reimbursements. *Becker's* reports that patients want to be able to use their portals to schedule appointments online, view lab and test results, view bills or make payments, check prescriptions or refills, and send email to staff (http://goo.gl/g8RnOu). This one will be useful at today's HITPC meeting.

The train ride from my apartment in Southwest Washington, DC, to my office in Silver Spring is usually a period of intermittent cellular connectivity, which I capitalize on to catch up on email without interruptions by phone calls or text messages. Today proved no different. Emails about new projects intermingled with the agenda for today's HITPC meeting and some ANA talking points. Mostly, my boss reminds me to respond to policymakers with remarks considerate of patients' needs and remain mindful of a nursing workload that prevents them from meeting those needs.

Another thing I like to remind policymakers to do is remain provider neutral. Nearly one-third of Medicare beneficiaries will receive care from an advance practice registered nurse (APRN; e.g., nurse practitioner or clinical nurse specialist) in any given year, so ONC and CMS ought to keep that in mind when making rules and regulations from laws that permit care from eligible professionals. These include APRNs and physician's assistants, among others. While APRNs might not legally benefit from the Medicare quality incentive programs, there is no reason to write them out of the rules and regulations set by ONC.

An overheard conversation on the train pertained to getting a "…doctor that takes Obamacare insurance." I don't interject. I just listen. Everything is knowledge that might inform today's or tomorrow's conversations. A good wonk knows how to remain purple, which is neither red nor blue, but independent. The Affordable Care Act and all other laws, regulations, and other policies related to healthcare are things that I need to know and understand, particularly as they pertain to implementation, maintenance, or evaluation. These policies affect patients, clinicians, payers, vendors, and the government. Whether they affect me is immaterial. My job is to use my skills and knowledge to inform the policies and learn from those who develop and implement them. When working for ANA, my lens is patient outcomes and nursing inputs. Remaining independent allows me to do my job effectively and in an unbiased way. I arrive at ANA headquarters by 7:30 a.m.

My desk is tidy in a violent sort of way. Things are in piles a week old. I usually straighten and start anew on Monday. I'm so glad it is not Monday. I am going to need this weekend. Among the piles, I see a brief I prepared on the implementation of ONC's BlueButton and Direct initiatives. The review for the two-page brief included a thorough read of the Department of Veterans Affairs (VA) website on the topic, ONC's Standards & Interoperability Framework wiki, Buzz Blogs, the BlueButton + style sheets, as well as reading analyses by HIMSS and *Becker's,* among others. It's interesting that association leadership—for that matter, all leaders—expect that a person can summarize hundreds of pages of regulation, analysis, and opinion into two pages. I did my level best. I spend five minutes chatting with my close colleague Maureen Dailey, RN, PhD, CWOCN. She is a Senior Policy Fellow, a noted expert on quality nursing care, and the reason I schlepped into the office before the meeting. She reminds me of a few important considerations before I leave.

I arrive in time to meet the (then) new National Coordinator, Dr. Karen DeSalvo, before the meeting starts. Ensuring that you get in front of public officials frequently, so that they know your name and whom you represent, is an important part of getting work done in this city. We engage in some polite conversation about her impending meeting with ANA's leadership. She seems excited—that's great news! She leaves me to take her seat at the head of the table for the first time. After the call to order, the Chair, Dr. Paul Tang, introduces her as co-chair. She makes some eloquent opening remarks, which includes her goals for the committee and the ONC.

After this, multitasking becomes the order of the day. While monitoring the meeting, I am still responsible for reviewing the latest update from the University of Kansas School of Nursing report on the development of the pressure ulcer electronic quality measure (eMeasure). This is the first eMeasure developed for the National Database of Nursing Quality Indicators (NDNQI). It might also be the first eMeasure currently implemented. Great people, like Drs. Nancy Dunton and Rosemary Kennedy, are developing and testing this incidence measure. So far, they have it implemented in two EHRs. The report and my reply with recommendations share time with the presenters' updates from CMS on EHR certification and Meaningful Use (MU) criteria. Robert Anthony of CMS mentions Direct addresses, which are essential for MU Stage 2 success. For MU Stage 2, providers must give patients a mechanism through which to view, download, and transmit (VDT) their health data in a secure way. This gains my full attention. Later, Drs. Tang and George Hripcsak update the committee on the work of the MU Workgroup. This, too, mentions VDT. I listen to this and take notes. I had not planned to make public comments, but today will be a good day to do that.

I have been tracking this committee, the Standards Committee, and the news from vendors regarding VDT for some time now. At this point, it is a great, but fledgling, idea. After the ONC Standards update comes the first opportunity for public comments. I stay silent. My ideas have not quite come together. I'll make my comments at the day's end. I spot an empty outlet, so I can charge my nearly dead laptop while I have lunch with colleagues. We have sandwiches while discussing VDT and standards. This is a great time to network, but I have to run back early to make an appointment to meet with Dr. Dailey at ANA headquarters after the meeting. Maureen and I will plan tomorrow's meetings with the ANA leadership team to update them on the eMeasure. It's 1:00 p.m. and the HITPC starts exactly on time.

The committee discusses privacy and security issues, including patient interactions. Kimberly Lynch presents an update on the work of the Regional Extension Centers, which give physicians and other eligible providers access to resources to achieve MU and obtain certified EHR technologies.

Finally, Michelle Consolazio, who keeps the meetings on track, calls for public comments. She gives commenters three minutes. I stand, walk to the table, and sit before the microphone looking directly at Dr. DeSalvo to make my comments on Direct addresses. You can find the transcript and audio at http://healthit.gov/facas/calendar/2014/01/14/hit-policy-committee.

No one responds. The committee never responds directly to the public. I leave the table and retake my seat. It is now 3:00 p.m. I spend a few moments chatting with colleagues, make my way to the front to reiterate my comments to Dr. DeSalvo, shake her hand, and leave for the train again. Very few people are on it, so I spend the time starting my meeting report to the leadership. I arrive at ANA headquarters again at 3:45 p.m.

It is such a pleasure to meet with Maureen. She is a knowledgeable nurse with the heart and soul of a New Yorker. Meetings are all business, until they are not. In either case, they move at a considerable pace. We chat a few minutes about our days and then tear into the eMeasure report. Things are going very well, which makes for a nice leadership report. After preparing a one-pager, we decide that we ought to write something about the eMeasure for *The American Nurse*, a monthly journal published by ANA. We plan to meet to discuss it later in the week. It's 5:30 p.m. and time to go home.

Update: Since I wrote this 'Day in the Life' entry, I left ANA to become a Senior Social Scientist for Econometrica, Inc., a federal contractor based in Bethesda, Maryland. The company implements, manages, and evaluates public policy instruments, including quality measures and health IT standards. The roles, while functionally different, are quite similar. In my current role, I implement and evaluate the effectiveness of policy as it affects clinicians and patients, but make no advocacy-based recommendations for policy. Essentially, these are just two different lenses focusing on the same outcomes: improvements in the processes and outcomes of healthcare. By the way, I heard that ONC might be postponing some of the VDT aspects of MU. They are also discussing how to simplify Direct addresses. I am not sure whether my comments affected that, but I think they might have contributed in some way.

Former Deputy National Coordinator, Office of the National Coordinator for Health IT

*Judy Murphy, RN, FACMI, FHIMSS, FAAN**

- **Years in Field:** 30
- **Years in Current Role:** 1
- **Education:** BSN, Nursing, Alverno College.

As Deputy National Coordinator for Programs and Policy at ONC, in the U.S. Department of Health & Human Services (HHS) in Washington, D.C., I led federal efforts to assist healthcare providers in adopting health IT to improve care and promote consumers' greater understanding and use of health IT for their own health. I was responsible for coordinating all of the HITECH (Health Information Technology for Economic and Clinincal Health) programs, part of the American Recovery and Reinvestment Act of 2009 (ARRA). These included:

- Regional Extension Center (REC) program
- State Health Information Exchange (HIE) program
- Beacon Community program
- Consumer eHealth program
- Workforce Development program
- EHR Certification program

Later, as Chief Nursing Officer at ONC, my federal role changed and I was responsible for coordinating all health IT-enabled quality policy and standards, integrating standardized clinical decision support into clinical practice, and improving the safety of health IT. In my essay here, I will highlight some of my experiences in both of those roles.

Internally, as with many leadership positions, I spent time managing staff and projects, and ensuring that there was harmony and consistency between the various teams and programs. I put in place project tracking and monitoring tools in order to define and measure deliverables, as well as ensure alignment with ONC and HHS strategic plans and annual goals. I built bridges between ONC's sometimes conflicting priorities for developing new policies and executing on existing programs. The Meaningful Use Program is an example of a policy-driven initiative, in which regulations are written governing the activities of the program. There is a very specific cadence for rule-making, with notification of proposed rules and public comment periods resulting in the publication of a final rule. In other cases, the ONC might convene stakeholders or coordinate activities, but let the industry take the lead making the necessary changes without regulation. It was always both a balancing act and a judgment call to determine when and where the government should intervene by setting policy versus letting the market drive the changes.

Externally, I coordinated ONC's work to "get down into the weeds" with EHR suppliers and healthcare providers, thus making it possible for citizens to benefit quickly from the incentive structures put into place under the HITECH Act. This often involved meetings with vendors, provider organizations, and industry and specialty organizations like the American Hospital Association (AHA), American Nurses Association (ANA), American Medical Association (AMA), American Academy of Family Physicians (AAFP), or American Association of Retired Persons (AARP). This outreach also often included presentations at meetings or conferences describing ONC's work, progress in the Meaningful Use program, and movement on achieving strategic goals. I also worked closely with ONC's federal advisory committees, the Health IT Policy and Standards Committees, to ensure the policy, regulatory, and non-regulatory vision for advancing the benefits of using health IT became a reality.

As with many organizations, the ONC needed to have our "feet on the ground and our eye on the prize"—essentially balancing current operational tasks with future planning and goals. Something I brought to the table here was my unique breadth and depth of health IT implementation experience over the previous 25 years. I had been in the trenches with my feet planted firmly on the ground, and I understood the many facets of EHR work, including vendor issues and clinical users' concerns. Additionally, I was responsible for the HITECH efforts at Aurora Health Care, where I helped shepherd half of their hospitals and eligible providers to achieve MU and receive EHR incentive payments in 2011. This helped my role at the ONC immensely, and gave me credibility both internally with staff and externally with stakeholders. I used my experience and nursing skills every single day in interpreting requirements and evaluating how EHRs are and should be used.

As a nurse, I know what it's like to be on the frontlines of patient care, whether in a physician's office, hospital, long-term care facility, rehabilitation clinic, or patient's home. I know what it's like not to have care continuity across the continuum or not to have the information you need at each transition of care. EHRs are installed in many of our healthcare venues; now the challenge at the national level is interoperability of those EHRs and getting health information exchanged between them in order to provide patient-centric care. Who better than a nurse to help coordinate the national foundation for health IT at ONC in order to build a 21st-century healthcare system?

---

* Ms. Murphy is currently Chief Nursing Officer & Director, Global Business Services, at IBM Healthcare.

Afterword

Willa Fields, RN, DNSc, FHIMSS

Health information technology (IT) and nursing informatics (NI) are continuously evolving as innovations are made, legislation is passed, and regulations are implemented. This evolution brings with it exciting opportunities for nurse informaticists to transform health and healthcare in the areas of service, administration, education, and research. As demonstrated in the HIMSS 2014 Nursing Informatics Workforce Survey,[1] nurse informaticists are crucial in the development, implementation, and optimization of health IT.

Ultimately, health IT will be interoperable and well integrated into our workflows. The Office of the National Coordinator for Health Information Technology (ONC) has embarked on a 10-year interoperability roadmap.[2] This roadmap will leverage health IT to improve health and healthcare while decreasing costs. Nurse informaticists have an opportunity to influence the direction of the roadmap through our unique perspective, from providing patient care to developing, implementing, and optimizing health IT. We can participate in ONC forums, listening sessions, and public comment activities. ONC has developed a wiki for ongoing dialogue and input about interoperability.[3] These ONC opportunities are available to all nurse informaticists, from novice to expert.

Career Opportunities

A nurse informaticist has clinical and technological knowledge and experience. Career opportunities abound throughout healthcare organizations. In the hospital, nurse informaticists have roles in both the information systems and nursing departments.[4] In information systems, nurse informaticists have roles such as Chief Information

Officer (CIO), Vice President/Director/Manager of clinical informatics teams, Project Manager, Trainer, and various types of analysts (e.g., Systems Analyst, Clinical Analyst, Nurse Analyst). In the nursing department, their roles include Chief Nursing Informatics Officer (CNIO), Vice President/Director/Manager of Nursing Informatics, Nurse Analyst, and Quality Analyst. Regardless of the title or department, nurse informaticists are vital in transforming healthcare through the optimum use of health IT.

Nurse informaticist career opportunities are as varied as nursing positions and exist in any organization that develops or utilizes health IT. For example, health IT software companies have multiple roles for nurse informaticists, including leadership positions (e.g., CNIO), Systems Analysts, and Trainers. Any organization with an electronic health record (EHR) needs a nurse informaticist to assist in the development, implementation, and optimization of the EHR. Nurse informaticists are employed by ambulatory care centers, retail clinics, public health departments, consulting firms, and health insurance companies. We are a major pillar of healthcare and a central decision maker.

With all of these nursing informatics opportunities, how do novice nurse informaticists begin? They do so with thorough preparation and networking.

Preparation

Here's my advice: in addition to obtaining advanced education in nursing informatics, become a certified nurse informaticist. Depending on your career goals and qualifications, three certifications are available. The American Nurses Credentialing Center (ANCC) offers board certification in Nursing Informatics for nurses with clinical and informatics experience.[5] The Healthcare Information and Management Systems Society (HIMSS) offers two types of informatics certification: Certified Associate in Healthcare Information and Management Systems (CAHIMS) and Certified Professional in Healthcare Information and Management Systems (CPHIMS).[6] The certified associate certification is for emerging professionals in health information management with fewer than five years of experience, whereas the certified professional certification is for more experienced informaticists with five or more years of experience. The HIMSS certifications are open to all professionals in healthcare informatics. The American Medical Informatics Association (AMIA) is developing an Advanced Interprofessional Informatics Certification for experienced informatics professionals.[7] This certification will be available in the next few years.

Networking

Network through professional organizations. Join an informatics specialty organization and meet other nurse informaticists (e.g., American Nursing Informatics Association [ANIA], AMIA, HIMSS). These organizations have national and regional conferences, and a variety of committees for participation. Other nursing organizations have informatics special interest groups, committees, and educational offerings.

Interview nurse informaticists about their own career development and ask for any advice they might have for you. Develop a mentoring relationship with a nurse informaticist. HIMSS offers career services for emerging informaticists and has a nursing eMentoring program through which you can get practical advice from established leaders in the field.[8]

In conclusion, I encourage you to pursue your professional dreams in nursing informatics. Opportunities are growing daily. An exciting and rewarding career awaits you. I know that has been my experience. And I hope it will be yours, too.

REFERENCES

1. HIMSS 2014 Nursing Informatics Workforce Survey. http://www.himss.org/ni-workforce-survey.
2. Office of the Coordinator for Health Information Technology. Connecting Health and Care for the Nation: A 10-Year Vision to Achieve an Interoperable Health IT Infrastructure. http://www.healthit.gov/sites/default/files/ONC10y-earInteroperabilityConceptPaper.pdf.
3. Nationwide Interoperability Roadmap Community Home. Sep 1, 2014. http://confluence.siframework.org/display/NIRCH/Nationwide+Interoperability+Roadmap+Community+Home.
4. Dieckhaus T. Nursing informatics practice in traditional hospital settings. *Nursing.* 2014; 44(10):18-20.

5. American Nurses Credentialing Center. Informatics Nursing. http://www.nurse-credentialing.org/InformaticsNursing.

6. HIMSS. Health IT Certification. http://www.himss.org/health-it-certification?navItemNumber=13588.

7. American Medical Informatics Association. Advanced Interprofessional Informatics Certification (AIIC) Program. http://www.amia.org/advanced-interprofessional-informatics-certification.

8. HIMSS. HIMSS eMentors. http://www.himss.org/health-it-career-services/e-mentors.

Chapter 1 Case Study

Career Options for Nurses Working with Informatics

Many nurses are intrigued by the idea of working in a position which integrates technology into healthcare. A tremendous need exists for nurses who understand clinical informatics in order to provide solutions to existing problems in the healthcare arena. How does a clinical nurse position his or herself in order to help meet this need and have a valuable career focusing on healthcare informatics?

Why Would a Nurse Want a Job in Informatics?

One must have a passion for healthcare informatics and not just use it as an escape to get out of doing hands-on patient care. The work can be hard, involve long hours, and include working shifts other than Monday through Friday during the day. On the bright side, nurses working with informatics can have the satisfaction of making a significant impact on the care of every patient in the organization, helping to provide safe, quality, and cost-effective care.

Positioning Oneself for a Job in Healthcare Informatics

Clinical expertise is a first requirement for working as an informatics nurse. It is not a good position for a new graduate who is not yet adept at the current workflow and knowledgeable about how it can be improved. The strength of an informatics nurse is his or her clinical experience coupled with knowledge of information technology (IT).

Assess your skills and strengths. Are you good at the technical aspects of IT? Do you have good communication, teaching, and conflict-resolution skills? Do you have knowledge of the organization in which you want to work, including the workflow and culture? Assess your ability to relocate or move. Not all jobs will be available in your home town. Do you want to work for a hospital or other healthcare facility, vendor, or consulting firm, or in an academic role?

Let others know about your desire to find a position that includes informatics. Networking is a key activity. Many positions are discovered by word of mouth and not in the mainstream job channels. One will never find this job in the local newspaper! Meet the employees of the IT department as well as Human Resources and understand what positions might be available.

Volunteer within the organization in which you are already known. You might volunteer to be a super user or to help test a system that is being implemented.

Take continuing education courses on topics related to nursing and healthcare informatics. Many in-person courses, online courses, and webinars are available on a variety of healthcare informatics topics. One program is the Nursing Informatics Boot Camp, which allows nurses to understand the depth and breadth of nursing informatics (NI) and help a nurse decide if informatics is the career to pursue. [The Nursing Informatics Boot Camp is a product of Newbold Consulting, Franklin, TN. NIBootCamp@comcast.net]

Membership in organizations like HIMSS (www.himss.org) is extremely important for education and networking. HIMSS offers a student rate which provides many of the same benefits of regular membership at a greatly reduced rate. HIMSS has a job board which can be searched to see what positions are available and the requirements for those positions.

Networking is key. If your organization has an informatics nurse, take him or her to lunch to interview him or her for ideas of what the role entails. If a position is available, that informatics nurse might think of letting you know about the job. Join any of the groups of the Alliance for Nursing Informatics (www.allianceni.org). Attend local, state, and national conferences in order to increase your education and find out what jobs are available. Many of the healthcare informatics organizations, like HIMSS, have nursing support groups and electronic mailing lists.

One might consider working with a recruiter to find a job in healthcare informatics. A recruiter will help with sample resumes, getting your resume in order, and positioning you for your first or next job in informatics.

Social networking sites such as LinkedIn may help in the job search. Search for leaders in NI, pay attention to what they put on their social media sites, and use that as a model.

Typical Positions

The first position a nurse may hold may be that of a super user within the organization. Sometimes one will volunteer for these positions or sometimes one is selected. This is a good reason why it is important to let others know of your interest in informatics. In this position, the super user may be trained on a particular software product, then will turn around and train others on his or her unit. The super users may be asked to test new products prior to the release of that product. One may do this job full time without patient assignments for a period of time, then later work part time as a super user and return to the previous patient care work as well.

The next job within the same organization might be that of a clinical analyst. In this role, one examines the current workflows of nurses and others and determines processes that allow for more efficient, effective, and safer patient care. One would attend meetings to customize or optimize specific software. One might be called upon to assist in selecting software, or training others on a product. This might be a stepping stone to work for a vendor installing software. Some nurses work for a consulting company to advise clients on any aspect of the system life cycle—assessment, planning, design, build, implementation, testing, evaluating, maintaining, and support systems.

Education in Nursing/Healthcare Informatics

Certification in NI is available through the American Nurses Credentialing Center for nurses who have experience as a nurse, at least one year of experience as an informatics nurse, and continuing education hours. If two nurses are applying for the same position, and all other credentials are the same, it is likely that certification could be the deciding factor to determine who gets the position.

A wide range of educational programs are available for NI. Many jobs in informatics do require a master's degree or higher. Some traditional brick and mortar or online programs offer certificates, a Master's degree, a post-Master's degree, a Doctor of Nursing Practice, or a Doctor of Philosophy (PhD) in NI. Holding a degree does not guarantee a job in informatics, but is a good idea for those who intend to work in the field. Programs at the Master's level typically include a practicum experience. Many have leveraged a practicum experience into a permanent position.

Nursing is a rewarding and varied career. Many opportunities exist for continuing that rewarding career by combining nursing and informatics.

Discussion Questions

1. In your environment, would it be preferable to report to Information Services (IS)/IT or the Nursing Department? Discuss the pros and cons.
2. Does the definition of NI incorporate those new to the profession of nursing? Justify your answer.
3. If you are just starting out in an NI role, which one (or more) of the functional areas of NI would be of interest to you? Defend your position.

Chapter 2 Case Study

Using Standards Development Processes to Establish Industry Baselines and Norms

Nursing informatics' short history has been characterized by revolutionary change and constant innovation. Emergent technologies have been introduced and have thrived or failed. Technologies from other industries have been adopted by nurses, such as when Sue Kinnick[1] observed the use of bar codes to expedite the return of her rental car and adopted the same technology to make the process of providing medications safer through bar code medication administration. Quick application and assimilation of new technologies are easier to implement on a small scale, but the real opportunity lies with broad industry adoption of common practices that allow for new knowledge about nursing or the human condition to be generated through large, similar data and information stores.

The ability to capture data about nursing practice and patient outcomes on a large scale has quickly advanced the body of knowledge generated by the discipline of nursing. Similar ideas, implemented in non-standard ways, slow down the opportunities for broad measurement, research and refinement of practices. Nurse informaticists have successfully used standards development processes to be able to drive consistent development of nursing terminologies, health IT functionality and data standards. The following case study traces the history of one standardization effort that was led by, or had participation of, a large number of nurse informaticists.

Background

In 2003, a public-private activity supported by the U.S. Department of Health & Human Services (HHS), Department of Veterans Affairs (VA), HIMSS, and the Robert Wood Johnson Foundation, asked Health Level Seven (HL7) to accelerate the work they were performing to develop a consensus-based standard for the functionality of an electronic health record (EHR).[2] This case study represents the activities of the HL7 Electronic Health Record Technical Committee from 2003 to today to illustrate how nurse informaticists can have historical impact on nursing practice and the broader healthcare industry. Nurses have always been part of the leadership of this highly influential technical committee. Other leaders have included physicians, industry leaders, and technologists.

When the HL7 EHR Technical Committee approached the problem, a number of similar but slightly different ideas existed throughout industry, domestically in the United States, but also internationally. The HL7 EHR Technical Committee could have limited their scope to move quickly to a final product, but knew that there was an international need for a common language by which to describe EHR functionality. The activity started with an international outreach to find others that were working on similar ideas. Once these activities were identified, negotiation toward consensus led to international cooperation on the work products. The final result is an internationally accepted standard that has been used domestically and internationally as a standard for a common language and framework for vendors, users, policymakers, and researchers.

Data/Research or Information for Reader

In 2000, the "best of breed" hospital IT systems were beginning to merge into seamless solutions called electronic health records. While many of these systems were deployed, there was not consensus on exactly what an EHR was or should be. How could the government give out incentives for their use? How could vendors communicate succinctly to users about their functions and how they exceeded industry norms? How could professional associations and health information management professionals communicate domain-specific needs for EHRs?

Domestic and international standards development organizations (SDOs) used varying language to describe EHRs. The American Society for Testing and Materials (ASTM) used electronic medical records (EMR); the International Organization for Standardization (ISO) used electronic health record systems (EHR-S); and HL7 used electronic health record (EHR), but had not yet created a formal standard for the term. Along with the conflict in naming, a lack of understanding existed regarding what was in scope and what was out of scope of an EHR system.

Challenges

Faced with international ambiguity, the HL7 EHR Technical Committee first sought coordination with other SDOs. Domestically, ASTM was not creating standards for EHR system functionality. Internationally, ISO was well underway building a standard for EHR-S Scope Definition and Context work. It was negotiated that HL7 would create functional standards and submit the work to ISO for inclusion into the ISO body of standards. In return, HL7 would adopt the ISO EHR system definitional work and not create redundant work.

The Institute of Medicine (IOM) was also working on a letter report entitled "Key Capabilities of an Electronic Health Record System: Letter Report." Through a coordinated effort, the IOM work informed the early work of the HL7 EHR Technical Committee while at the same time, the work of HL7 was considered a significant input to the IOM work and was thus acknowledged.[3]

Decisions/Actions

Once the broader scope was negotiated and decided upon across SDOs and others, the detailed work began. The team at HL7 wanted to create a functional model that provided a language by which users, vendors, researchers, policymakers and others could speak about EHR systems. But any EHR system would be a subset of available functions.

Each function includes a 'Function ID,' 'Function Name,' 'Function Statement,' 'Function Description,' 'Examples' of the function, the ability to link the function to similar functions by a 'See Also' field and 'Conformance Criteria.' The original EHR-S FM contained approximately 130 functions; the current Release 2 of the EHR-S FM contains approximately 300 functions.

The functions are arranged into seven chapters, as depicted in **Figure 1-A.**

While the EHR-S FM has a high level of specificity about functions, few, if any practice sites will require all functions. The team created the ability for users to rate each function with 'Shall,' 'Should,' or 'May,' which allowed the user to indicate required (Shall), desirable (Should), or optional (May) functionality. This has led to communities of practice to gather and create practice-specific profiles which are freely available at www.hl7.org.

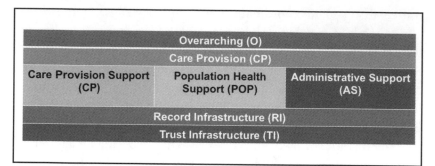

Figure 1-A: Sections of the HL7 Electronic Health Record System Functional Model, Release 2. (From Health Level Seven® International. Used with Permission.)

An example of a Care Provision function and its sub (child) functions are depicted in **Figure 2-A**.

Care Provision			Example child functions:	
	CP.1	Manage Clinical History		
	CP.2	Render Externally-sourced Information	CP.1	**Manage Clinical History**
	CP.3	Manage Clinical Documentation	CP.1.1	Manage Patient History
	CP.4	Manage Orders	CP.1.2	Manage Allergy, Intolerance and Adverse Reaction List
	CP.5	Manage Results	CP.1.3	Manage Medication List
	CP.6	Manage Treatment Administration	CP.1.4	Manage Problem List
	CP.7	Manage Future Care	CP.1.5	Manage Strengths List
	CP.8	Manage Patient Education & Commu	CP.1.6	Manage Immunization List
	CP.9	Manage Care Coordination & Reporti	CP.1.7	Manage Medical Equipment, Prosthetic/Orthotic, Device List
Details for functions are arranged in a hierarchical fashion			CP.1.8	Manage Patient and Family Preferences

Figure 2-A: Care Provision Function. (From Health Level Seven® International. Used with Permission.)

Outcomes, Lessons Learned

International collaboration allowed for learning from global best practices and promulgation of this work with the international SDO community. Now that the work is published, those that work internationally are able to use this common framework. For example, vendors that are responding to requests for services or certification guidelines from different countries will find a similar language and expectation of EHR-S functionality that does not need to be modified dramatically for each country within which they work.

The interdisciplinary nature of the team led to a comprehensive model which describes an EHR-S for all users.

Early coordination with multiple domestic and international SDOs resulted in recognition of the work being undertaken by HL7, and allowed for inclusion of the HL7 work into other SDOs. This has resulted in the acceleration of complementary work as multiple SDOs are not put in the position of promulgating their unique functional standards, as has been seen with health IT interoperability messaging standards. Today, coordination of this work takes place across six different SDOs.[4]

The HL7 EHR Technical Committee has stayed current with technology trends over more than the last decade, and has expanded their work to include new technologies as they have become more prevalent. Community of interest involvement has significantly impacted the expansion of the original EHR-S scope to include personal health records (PHRs).

Conclusion

NI leadership was critical to this formalized effort to bridge the users of health IT systems and the systems themselves. Because nurse informaticists were positioned in leadership roles at HL7, they were able to have significant influence over the creation of this functional standard. In addition, the two nurses who sequentially co-chaired the HL7 EHR Technical Committee were also peer-voted to be Directors at Large of the HL7 Board of Directors. This further expanded the NI influence on the development of health IT standards. While nurse informaticists were instrumental in leading the international standardization of functional models for EHR systems, this is just one example of the many efforts nurse informaticists have led to standardize the NI specialty, the domain of nursing and the healthcare sector.

Discusion Questions

1. Nursing informatics' history has many examples of similar ideas arising at the same time. What are some of those?
2. When similar ideas have arisen, what has been the progression?
3. What have been the advantages to the NI profession of this push towards standardization?
4. What were some of the professional skills exhibited by the nurse informaticists who co-chaired this effort?

REFERENCES

1. Wood D. RN's Visionary Bar Code Innovation Helps Reduce Medication Errors. NurseZone.com; 2003. www.nursezone.com/nursing-news-events/devices-and-technology/rn%E2%80%99s-visionary-bar-code-innovation-helps-reduce-medication-errors_24580.aspx.
2. HL7 EHR System Functional Model: A Major Development Towards Consensus on EHR System Functionality. White Paper. Health Level Seven; 2004. www.hl7.org/documentcenter/public_temp_341B3F50-1C23-BA17-0C595FB8F34D4F75/wg/ehr/EHR-SWhitePaper.pdf.
3. Key Capabilities of an Electronic Health Record System: Letter Report. Washington, DC: National Academies Press; 2003. www.nap.edu/openbook.php?record_id=10781&page=30.
4. HL7 EHR-System Functional Model, Release 2. Health Level Seven International; Apr, 2014. www.hl7.org/implement/standards/product_brief.cfm?product_id=269.

Chapter 3 Case Study

Using Kaizen to Improve Workflow and Clinical Documentation Post-EHR Implementation

A healthcare system has implemented a new EHR in a multi-hospital environment. The design, build, testing and implementation for this phased project was completed over two years and considered by the software vendor to be a very aggressive timeline. It becomes evident as the organization lifts itself out of the implementation phase that there are areas of workflow concerns and clinical documentation issues or defects that need to be addressed. Subject-matter experts representing all five hospitals, ambulatory care areas and emergency care centers, as needed, are invited to participate in Kaizen (the practice of continuous improvement) events to review the 10 most common workflows. The goal is to identify the areas for improvement and create a new workflow that would maximize efficiency and improve patient safety and outcomes. This case study will reflect a Kaizen to evaluate the STEMI (ST segment elevation myocardial infarction) patient that presents at a hospital or emergency care center that does not have a cardiac cath lab.

Background

At this health system, the process for reporting issues is by calling customer support, which is available 24/7, or by contacting the assigned nurse informatics analyst. Some end users will contact the EHR build team analyst directly, though it is discouraged. Due to the number of issue tickets created related to the STEMI workflow, it was selected as the first Kaizen to occur. During the design phase of the EHR implementation, the cardiac cath labs at the three hospitals had difficulty standardizing their practices. This became evident after go-live when workarounds began to evolve. The need to document a workflow mapping through a Kaizen Lean process was established.

The event was scheduled over two full days and was facilitated by a Lean Specialist and the Director of Informatics, and was sponsored by the Chief Nurse and Chief Medical Information Officers. Participants included Emergency Department (ED) physicians, ED nurses, Registration, Unit Secretaries, Cath Lab techs, Cath Lab nurses, Cardiology, Cardiac Critical Care nurses, Bed Placement Coordinators, Nurse Informatics Analysts and Application Build Analysts. Day One included current state workflow mapping. Each workflow step was placed into one of five categories: Non-EHR Process Step, EHR Process Step, Non-EHR Issue Opportunity, EHR Issue Opportunity, or Patient Action Step. (See **Figure 1-B**).

During Day Two, participants identified three primary areas/clusters where error or issues occur. These areas were then listed in a table format for the participants to evaluate the issues' affect. Using a scale of one to five, on a Patient Safety (x-axis) and also its affect on End User Efficiency (y-axis), the facilitator mapped each issue on a grid. Once the issues were scored, they were then listed in order from highest to lowest. Once ranked, the Application Build Analysts and representatives from the EHR vendor assisted the group in reviewing the EHR Process Steps and EHR Issue/Opportunities. They were critical in the expectation setting of whether the issue/opportunity could be fixed/enhanced using the current state EHR platform, or if it would have to wait for the system enhancements that would be included in the upgrade to occur within the next 12 months.

Assessment

The Kaizen workflow mapping determined there were currently 32 sequential steps and 87 steps in total within the workflow. As many as six steps were occurring simultaneously by the 11 end-user roles involved.

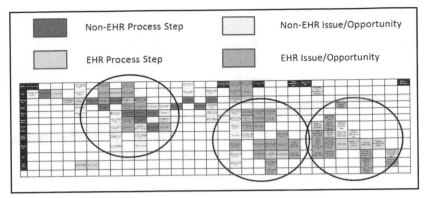

Figure 1-B. Current state workflow mapping.

The Kaizen participants, Build Team analysts and EHR representatives determined that within the top 11 issues, there were three for which the Training Team and Informatics Analysts would provide additional education to improve compliance with the existing workflow while using existing tools. Only two items would require waiting for the upgrade to have the functionality needed for the change, which left six items for immediate resolution optimizing the current EHR System (see **Table 1-B**).

Table 1-B. Top issues for education and support.

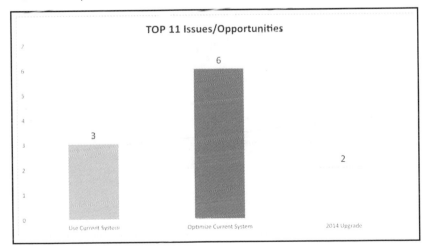

Recommendation

All 11 items were assigned owners. The six Optimize Current System items identified by the Kaizen participants were assigned to the Application Build Team to resolve. The three Use Current System items were given to the Training Team to create tip sheets that were given to the Informatics Analysts for distribution and end-user support. The two items that would not be possible until the upgrade were placed on the "To Do" list for the appropriate Application Teams.

Discussion Questions

1. Were the appropriate roles selected to participate in this Kaizen event? Was anyone excluded?
2. What questions could have been asked during the Kaizen, or what could have occurred post-Kaizen to improve the outcomes and/or experience?

Chapter 4 Case Study

Healthcare Analytics—An Evolutionary Process

In 2010, the Clinical Informatics Team at the University of California-Irvine (UCI), was challenged to develop an analytics program that would address the clinical, operations, quality and research needs of the organization. The solution not only had to meet the immediate needs, but also had to meet future, yet unknown organizational needs.

The Clinical Informatics Team included a neuroscientist, three nurse informaticists, four programmers and a biostatistician. The extended team included a development partner with expertise in the technology selected, staff from operations, clinicians, staff from Quality and researchers. At the time, the organization did not have a cohesive analytics strategy, nor did they have a data repository or data visualization applications outside of spreadsheets.

Discussion

An initial assessment of the needs of all stakeholders was conducted. Face-to-face interviews and focus group sessions were conducted with over 50 members of the organization. Stakeholders included clinicians, staff from operations, staff from Quality and researchers. Significant findings from these interviews included the following:

- The organization's primary analytic platform was spreadsheets.
- No data governance structure was in place.
- Data acquisition was a manual process as there was no means of electronic data extraction.
- No one source of truth existed and there were many duplicative manual reports with conflicting data.
- Researches spent an inordinate amount of time gathering data for research.

- Staff from Quality spent 15 days per month gathering data and the other five days creating spreadsheets visualizing the data collected. This left very little time for quality improvement projects.

With this information in hand, as well as the mandate for both an immediate and long-term solution, the team decided on an evolutionary approach to data analytics. By evolving the solution over time, immediate, intermediate and future analytic needs of the organization could be met. Before starting the data evolution process, certain foundational work was conducted. This work included the following:

- Initiating a data governance model.
- Developing a data dictionary of all data elements used in organizational reports and dashboards; included in the data dictionary was the location in the EHR or in the paper record of all data elements.
- Ontological rightsizing by a thorough assessment and development of a plan for ensuring ontological correctness of data elements.

Once the fundamentals were addressed, the team started the healthcare analytics evolution shown in **Figure 1-C**. Using the Quality Team as an example, we see the first stage was the use of spreadsheets to collect and analyze quality data. At this stage, quality data was accumulated in spreadsheets via manual abstraction of quality data from such sources as paper documentation, the EHR and other healthcare systems. The folks in Quality spent approximately 15 days on data collection and analysis and had limited time to produce data visualizations in the form of reports that are then emailed, posted in SharePoint, or distributed at departmental meetings. After analysis of the quality data was completed, 30 days had passed, leaving very little time for quality improvement projects as the cycle then repeated itself.

In stage 2, we introduced a data visualization application to the spreadsheet. This one addition to the technology stack reaped many benefits. First, by using a data visualization application to build quality dashboards and making them accessible via a portal, we then had a means for members of the healthcare organization to view and interact with the quality dashboards. Second, the work of manually creating visualizations each month was eliminated because once the quality visualizations were built, there was no need to do this work again.

In stage 3, we added a data mart to the mix. In our Quality example, this would be a quality data mart. The advantage there is that we were now using data coming directly from the EHR and other healthcare systems, thus decreasing the workload of abstraction. Additionally, as the data was fed to the data mart daily, we then had dashboards that were close to real time.

In stage 4, we saw the introduction of a Big Data ecosystem comprising real-time EHR feeds, as well as data from other healthcare systems, devices in the hospital and at home, social media, open data, health information exchange (HIE), and population management systems (PMS). Abstraction for the Quality Team was minimal: we now had real-time alerts around quality and best of all, our quality peers were now freed up and had time for quality improvement projects.

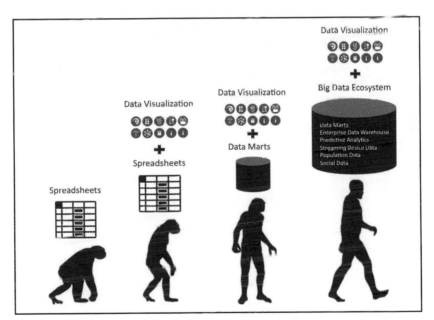

Figure 1-C: Healthcare Analytics' Evolution.

Recognizing that in stage 4 the team would be introducing a "Big Data" solution and at the time there was little use of Big Data technologies in healthcare, the team looked outside of healthcare for solutions. After conducting research and analyzing the technologies behind Facebook, LinkedIn, Twitter and Yahoo, it was decided to use the same technologies that powered those applications. **Figure 2-C** is a representation of the Modern Healthcare Platform developed by the Clinical Informatics Team. As the team was not experienced in these technologies, a development partner was brought in to build the Big Data platform. This was helpful for two reasons, the first being speed (the solution was built over a reasonable amount of time), and second, knowledge transfer (the Clinical Informatics Team worked side by side with the development partner to ensure their ownership and knowledge of the solution).

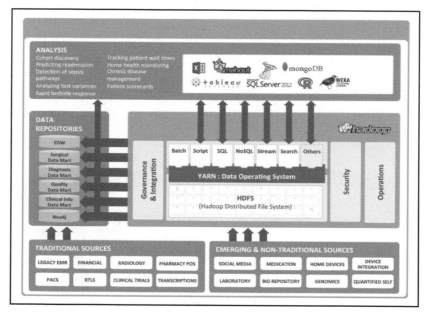

Figure 2-C: Modern Healthcare Platform.

The Modern Healthcare Platform allowed the organization to ingest data from any source including
- EMR
- Legacy data
- Physiological monitoring data
- Ventilator data
- Ancillary system data

- Home and wearable device data
- Social media data
- Omics data

Functionality developed within the platform included:

- Real-time monitoring of patient condition
- Integration of wearable and home monitoring data
- Predictive analytics
- Registries
- Cohort discovery
- Social media analytics
- Event notification

The evolutionary approach for delivering functionality iteratively was a success. Within 90 days the Quality Team had a visualization tool that removed the monthly tedium of developing a dashboard within the spreadsheet application. This alone gave the Clinical Informatics Team organizational credibility. Organizations are not receptive to long, drawn-out analytics projects that do not deliver functionality for months. Keeping the stakeholders informed throughout the process is essential. A breakdown in communication occurred when it came to the Big Data platform. Little was communicated early on, leading to confusion regarding the functionality of the EHR versus the Big Data platform.

Looking outside of healthcare for technologies that successfully deliver functionality was also successful. There is much to learn from other industries and how they utilize technology.

CONCLUSION

The analytics evolution at UCI was successful in a large part by employing an iterative solution that provided value from the first deployment of technology. How would you go about deploying an iterative technology solution, keeping in mind the need to deliver value early on? Although the initial communication to the organization was sound, the communication around the Big Data platform was not, leading to confusion by many of the stakeholders. For your organization, what might a sustainable communication model look like? It cannot be overstated how important the fore-mentioned foundational work was to the project. How would you obtain organizational buy-in for establishing a data governance model, creating a data dictionary and ensuring data consistency throughout the organization?

Discussion Questions

1. What is your strategy for ensuring that you keep up to date on emerging technologies?
2. Why do we want to avoid a System 2 response when visualizing operational data?
3. What does the nurse informaticist have to offer a vendor considering development of a population management application?

Acronyms Used in This Book

AACN	American Association of Colleges of Nursing
AAFP	American Academy of Family Physicians
AARP	American Association of Retired Persons
ACO	accountable care organization
AFMC	Arkansas Foundation for Medical Care
AHA	American Hospital Association
AHRQ	Agency for Healthcare Research and Quality
AIIC	Advanced Interprofessional Informatics Certification
AMA	American Medical Association
AMIA	American Medical Informatics Association
ANA	American Nurses Association
ANCC	American Nurses Credentialing Center
ANI	Alliance for Nursing Informatics
ANIA	American Nursing Informatics Association
APRN	Advanced Practice Registered Nurse
ARRA	American Recovery and Reinvestment Act of 2009
AS	administrative support
ASTM	American Society for Testing and Materials
BSN	Bachelor of Science in Nursing
BPA	best practice alert
CAHIMS	Certified Associate in Healthcare Information and Management Systems
CAP	College of American Pathologists
CCAN	Council on Computer Applications in Nursing
CI	clinical intelligence
CIO	chief information officer
CMIO	chief medical information officer
CMS	Centers for Medicare & Medicaid Services
CNIO	chief nursing informatics officer, or chief nursing information officer
CNO	chief nursing officer

COPs	Cooperatives of Practice
CP	care provision
CPHIMS	Certified Professional in Healthcare Information and Management Systems
CPOE	computerized provider order entry
CPT	Current Procedural Terminology (code set)
CRM	Crew Resource Management
CT	Clinical Terms (as in SNOMED Clinical Terms)
CTO	chief technology officer
DNP	Doctor of Nursing Practice
DSRIP	Delivery System Reform Incentive Program
ED	emergency department
EH	eligible hospital
EHR	electronic health record
EP	eligible professional
ETL	extract, transform and load
FQHC	Federally Qualified Healthcare Clinics
FTE	full-time equivalent
GSW	Georgia Southwestern State University
HDFS	Hadoop distributed file system
HIE	health information exchange
HHC	Home Health Care Classification
HHS	U.S. Department of Health & Human Services
HIMSS	Healthcare Information and Management Systems Society
HIS	health information services
HITECH	Health Information Technology for Economic and Clinical Health Act
HITPC	Health IT Policy Committee
HL7	Health Level Seven
HMO	health maintenance organization
HPC	high performance computing
ICD	International Classification of Diseases
ILN	Inova Learning Network
IN	informatics nurse
INS	informatics nurse specialist
IOM	Institute of Medicine
IS	information services

ISO	International Organization for Standardization
IT	Information technology
LTC	long-term care
MSN	Master of Science in Nursing
MU	Meaningful Use
NANDA	North American Nursing Diagnosis Association (Taxonomy)
NDNQI	National Database of Nursing Quality Indicators
NI	nursing informatics
NIC	Nursing Intervention Classification
NIH	National Institutes of Health
NLM	National Library of Medicine
NLP	natural language processing
NIS	nursing information system
NLN	National League for Nursing
NMDS	Nursing Minimum Data Set
NOC	Nursing Outcomes Classification
NP	nurse practitioner
NPO	nothing by mouth
ONC	Office of the National Coordinator for Health Information Technology
O	overarching
PCMH	patient-centered medical home
PCORI	Patient Centered Outcomes Research Institute
PDCA	Plan-Do-Check-Act process
PhD	Doctor of Philosophy
PHR	personal health record
PMA	population management application
PMI	Project Management Institute
PMP	Project Management Professional
PMS	population management system
POP	population health support
PPACA	Patient Protection and Affordable Care Act (also known as 'Obamacare')
QIN-QIO	Quality Innovation Network – Quality Improvement Organization
REC	regional extension center
RFP	request for proposal
RI	record infrastructure

RN	Registered Nurse
RN-BC	Registered Nurse-Board Certified (in a particular specialty)
RTLS	real-time location service
SBAR	Situation, Background, Assessment and Recommendation technique
SCAMC	Symposium on Computer Applications in Medical Care
SDO	standards development organization
SNF	skilled-nursing facilities
SNOMED RT	Systemized Nomenclature of Medicine Reference Terminology®
SQL	Structured Query Language
STEMI	ST segment elevation myocardial infarction
TIGER	Technology Informatics Guiding Education Reform
TTUHSC	Texas Tech University Health Sciences Center
UCI	University of California-Irvine
UK	United Kingdom
UMLS	Unified Medical Language System® (UMLS® Metathesaurus)
USPHS	U.S. Public Health Service
VA	U.S. Department of Veterans Affairs
VDT	view, download and transmit
VP	vice president
VoIP	voice over Internet protocol

Index